Preparing for His Glory

Preparing for His Glory

by
Mark Brazee

MBM Publications
Broken Arrow, Oklahoma

Unless otherwise indicated, all Scripture quotations are taken from the *King James Version* of the Bible.

Preparing for His Glory
First Printing 1993
ISBN 0-934445-02-8
Copyright © 1993 by Mark Brazee Ministries
P. O. Box 1870
Broken Arrow, Oklahoma 74013

Published by MBM Publications

Printed in the United States of America.

Table of Contents

Chapter 1
Beholding His Glory

Have you ever wondered about the miraculous revivals of the early 1900s? How could every bar in a single town close down, or every person in a service be healed? What caused such glorious manifestations of God?

I realized the answer to these questions was greatly related to the subject of the glory of God, so I began to study the glory. I asked many questions, like: What is the glory? What produces the glory? What does the glory do? Is it only in the Old Testament? Is the glory of God available for the Church today?

Signs Follow the Word

My first experience with the glory was so impressive that I told the Lord, "I'm willing to pay any price to learn to cooperate with it."

When I graduated from Bible school, I traveled on a ministry crusade team. I worked the book table, worked the prayer lines, and ran the sound equipment. Whatever needed to be done, I did it!

Our first meeting was a camp meeting in the Detroit, Michigan area. Fifteen hundred to two thousand people filled a tent on the parking lot of a large hotel.

About the fourth night of the meetings, the minister said, "The Spirit of God has been dealing with me to minister on the glory of God," and he proceeded to minister on the glory, telling about people whose lives had been changed by God's glory. Up until this time, the only thing I knew about the glory was that we weren't supposed to take any!

The minister gave Old and New Testament examples of the glory, and told of many different times it had manifested in his meetings. He told of times he had seen the glory come rolling into a service like a cloud and envelop the entire congregation.

Other times it would manifest like a giant flash bulb and every sinner in the building would suddenly find themselves at the altar to be saved, or at times everyone in the building would be instantly healed.

Then the minister asked people who wanted prayer for healing to come forward. My job was to help organize the healing line. He began to lay hands on people, and suddenly the Presence of God fell like I had never sensed it fall before. It seemed to fill the entire tent.

When the glory of God was in manifestation like that, the minister backed up a step and ran the full length of the prayer line. As he did, everyone in the prayer line almost simultaneously fell under the power of God.

There were so many people falling all around me, I could not catch them all! It reminded me of Saul of Tarsus' encounter with God's glory on the Damascus Road when he later said, ". . . *we were all fallen to the earth . . .*" (Acts 26:14).

People were healed, delivered, and changed by the power of God all over the building. I had never seen anything like this. At the end of his message, this minister gave an altar call, and many people flooded to the altar and were born again and filled with the Holy Ghost.

I told the Lord, "I do not understand what happened,

but if this is available for everyone, I want it — not for me, but to meet the needs of the people."

The Glory Falls in Colorado

One year later, I was a youth pastor for the next 13 months at a church in Colorado. During that time, we rented a lodge and held a youth camp in the mountains. Many teenagers attended the camp. The local high school football coach was a member of the church, and he went along as a chaperone.

One night we asked if he would share with the young people. He exhorted them with an anointed message about living right and serving God.

When he finished, several teens began to make fresh dedications of their lives to God. Then all of a sudden the glory of God fell. It was like Heaven came down to the earth. I sensed the same strong Presence of God that I had sensed in that other meeting when the glory fell. For two hours, the young people praised God and stayed in His Presence.

As the glory of God filled the room, I wandered around like I was in a fog that could not be seen with the natural eyes. I walked by one young man, who was 13 years old. I knew him, yet I did not know that he was not filled with the Holy Spirit.

I heard myself say to him, "You've never been filled with the Holy Ghost, have you?"

He replied, "No, I haven't." I barely touched his forehead, and he immediately started speaking in tongues.

A young girl who had broken her finger in an athletic activity that week was praising God. I walked by her and touched her finger. When I looked back at her, I saw her yank the splint off and bend her finger with her eyes open wide in surprise. She was instantly healed!

That one service changed many young people's lives. Many of those teenagers are now in the full-time ministry. The glory of God rested on those young people even into the next day.

People are never the same once they have experienced the glory of God.

The Glory Continues

Six months later, I went back to work for the other ministry where I had previously worked, as the manager and minister for Faith's Creation, a traveling singing group. One night, the group ministered in song at a church and I ministered the Word, gave an altar call, and prayed for the sick.

As I gave the microphone back to the pastor and returned to my seat, he said, "God has been dealing with me all day to pray for these young people." He prayed for all of us, and the Spirit of God began to move. The service continued for about two hours. The power of God was so strong that much of the time it was difficult to stand up.

At one point, the pastor walked by me, and I could not stand up. My mind was saying, "Don't do this!" but my body was saying, "I can't help it!" I felt so foolish, but I could not stand up; I spent half the evening on the floor. I was so drunk in the Holy Ghost that I could not even speak properly (Acts 2:4; Eph. 5:18).

Toward the end of the service, the pastor who was on the platform, said to an usher, "Please get me that box," pointing to a box full of prayer cloths. Then he quoted Acts 19:11-12: *"And God wrought special miracles by the hands of Paul: So that from his body were brought unto the sick handkerchiefs or aprons, and the diseases departed from them, and the evil spirits went out of them."*

People brought the Apostle Paul handkerchiefs, and when the anointing was in manifestation, he laid hands on the cloths, and people were healed as the handkerchiefs were laid upon their bodies. The anointing breaks the yoke of bondage (Isa. 10:27). Paul did not do the miracles; God did.

I was sitting on the front row when the pastor said, "Mark, come up here. Let's both lay hands on these cloths. The anointing is strong; we need to pray over these now."

We laid hands on the cloths, and again a wave of the glory of God swept through the church. As it did, we both fell from the platform onto the floor, the prayer cloths scattering everywhere.

The anointing was so strong, I thought, *If I needed healing, I sure would get one of those cloths right now.* I did not see the glory, but I knew the glory of God was in that place.

The Woman in the Wheelchair

A few years later, this same minister and I held a joint meeting in another church. I took the morning services, and he took the evenings. A woman who looked to be in her eighties attended the services every night with her daughter. This elderly woman glowed with the love of God. She was in a wheelchair, and her hands were twisted like they were arthritic.

During the Wednesday night service, this other minister began to pray for the sick. The anointing was so tangible that you could feel it as it swept into the room, and you could sense it getting stronger and stronger.

At the close of one of the services, the daughter pushed her mother in the wheelchair down the middle aisle for prayer. This minister was ready to lay hands on her when he looked up at me and said, "The anointing is on you, too, Mark. Come over here; let's double-team the devil."

I felt like I was walking through something tangible, the Presence of God was so strong. We reached out to pray for her, and both of us hit the floor backwards. We could not stand up in that Presence. We both tried to get up and lay hands on her, but we fell again.

Finally, someone held the other minister up while I crawled over on my knees and grabbed the chair. We laid hands on her and prayed. Soon the glory lifted, and I returned to my seat.

The other minister continued to lay hands on the rest of the people. The daughter turned the wheelchair around, and with her mother still in it, pushed the wheelchair back to her seat.

A minute or two later, we heard some commotion in the back. I turned around and saw this elderly woman walking down the aisle with her hands raised, praising God. She got up out of that chair and walked away perfectly whole. She received her healing in the Presence of the glory.

God Will Finish What He Starts

Several years ago, we held a four-night meeting at a church, and on the Wednesday night service, we ministered on healing. I planned to tell the people to wait until the next night to receive prayer for healing. But when I got ready to close the service, the Spirit of God prompted me to call anyone up who needed healing.

Many people lined up, and everyone in the line began to raise their hands and worship God. The Presence of God grew stronger, and the glory of God began to manifest. The anointing was strong.

I said, "Lord, You started this, so You finish it. I'm staying out of the way. Tell me if You want me to do anything."

Then the tangible Presence of God fell. I never prayed for one person, but people were healed everywhere. I was ready to close the service when the Spirit of God told me to call out one woman and lay hands on her, which I was hesitant to do.

This was the fifth service that this woman had attended, including Sunday morning and evening. The word of knowledge had operated a number of times, and no matter what ailment I called out by the Spirit, she came up and said she needed healing in that area.

I had prayed for her Sunday, Monday, and Tuesday, but she hadn't received anything. When I laid hands on her, I felt like I was laying hands on a brick wall.

The more you lay hands on people without them knowing how to receive, the further you can drive them from their healing. The first time they have hands laid on them, they hope they will be healed. Then after several attempts, you can almost hear them thinking as they come down the aisle, *I know it won't work, but I'll try anyway.*

This may not always be their fault. Sometimes ministers pray and lay hands on people over and over again without ever investigating *why* the people are not receiving their healing. My hesitancy was legitimate. I did not want to hinder her faith.

This woman came up to receive prayer, and I said, "I don't know why, but the Spirit of God told me to lay hands on you." I merely brushed her forehead, and she fell down under the power of God. When she got up, she was so drunk in the Holy Ghost that several people had to help her home.

The following night we held a testimony service. We discovered that more people were healed that one night than were healed the whole week. But this woman was the only person we laid hands on!

She reported, "I want you to know, there's not one symptom left in my body!" and she went back to her seat. Even though she had come up for prayer several times, she was finally able to receive her healing when the glory of God came into that service.

The Right Ingredients

Since that time, I have learned some things that have helped me to understand more about how the glory of God works. One thing I've learned is that results from God equal a ratio of anointing to faith. Let's say that to get healed it takes a percentage of faith plus a percentage of anointing to equal one-hundred-percent results.

For example, if you only have twenty percent faith, then it takes eighty percent of the anointing to make up the difference. If you have thirty percent faith, it will only require seventy percent of the anointing to get results. If you have fifty percent faith, it takes fifty percent of the anointing to get healed.

The more anointing that is present and in manifestation, the less faith it takes to receive from God. If you have a one-hundred-percent anointing, that's when the gifts of the Spirit manifest.

I've seen people receive things they were not believing for or expecting when the gifts of the Spirit were in operation. It clearly was not their faith. Faith believes before it sees and feels. These people barely believed it *after* seeing and feeling.

What happens is that many times people develop their faith doing all they can do, but they have only, let's say, thirty percent faith. They get in a service with thirty percent anointing, and they have thirty percent faith, and there's a lack of forty percent to be able to receive.

If we could get enough anointing to meet people where they are, we would get people healed who cannot seem to get healed any other way. For some reason this lady could not get her faith stretched to get her healing. But when we had a service where God was free to pour His glory out, she was able to receive her healing.

Probably the greatest manifestation you will ever see is the glory of God. The power of God was so strong that God met her where she was, and she was instantly healed.

You may know people who are doing all they know to do and are still not getting healed. It's not necessarily because of some deep, dark hidden sin in their life. For some reason, they are not making contact with the power of God.

We need services where the glory will get so strong that God will be able to reach people who have trouble making contact with the power of God.

I'm not minimizing the importance of the Word of God. But there are times God wants to come in and *confirm* His Word with signs following.

He wants to confirm His Word, not just by preaching and teaching, but also in demonstration of the Spirit and of power so that our faith might not stand in the wisdom of man, but in the power of God (1 Cor. 2:4,5).

Greater Glory Is Coming

One way the power of God is manifested is in the glory of God. Haggai 2:9 says, *"The glory of this latter house shall be greater than of the former, saith the Lord of hosts. . . ."*

You could interpret this scripture several different ways, and they would all be correct. But one way to interpret it is to say that the New Testament house of God is greater than the Old Testament house of God.

What does the "house of God" mean? In the Old Testament, it was a Temple made with hands where the Presence of God dwelt in the Holy of Holies. The Presence of God dwelt in the Old Testament Temple.

When Jesus died, the veil into the Holy of Holies where the Presence of God dwelt was torn in two, and God changed His Temple from one made with hands to one not made with hands. God put His Presence in us as believers and made His Presence available to us. That's when the house of God changed from an external building to the spirits of born-again believers.

Paul said to the Corinthians, *"Know ye not that ye are the temple of God, and that the Spirit of God dwelleth in you?"* (1 Cor. 3:16).

God must be a God of faith because He puts His Presence — the Presence that dwelt in the Holy of Holies — in us the minute we are born again.

The "house of God" in the New Testament is the Body of Christ, the Church. Born-again Christians are the "house" of God. God lives in us individually and corporately.

So we could interpret Haggai 2:9 this way: The glory of the last days of the Church is going to be greater than the glory of the first days of the Church.

So the closer we get to the last days, the stronger we can expect to experience the power of God. Whole churches and even whole cities will be changed by the glory of God. The glory of God is coming, but the Body of Christ has to prepare for this outpouring.

A Divine Personality

What is the glory of God? It's more accurate, however, to ask, "Who is the glory of God?" The glory of God is the Spirit of God — when He brings His very Presence in our midst.

We see this more clearly in the Book of Romans. Romans 6:4 says, ". . . *Christ was raised up from the dead by the glory of the Father. . . .*" Romans 8:11 says, *"But if the Spirit of him that raised up Jesus from the dead dwell in you. . . ."*

Both verses were written in the same letter, by the same author, to the same Christians. One verse said that the *glory* of God raised Jesus from the dead, and the other said that the Spirit of God raised Jesus from the dead. So *who* is the glory of God? *The glory of God is the Spirit of God.*

Old Testament Glory: Moses Longed To See God

Throughout the Word, we see examples where God manifested Himself — His glory — on this earth. For example, in Exodus 33:18, Moses said, *". . . I beseech thee, shew me thy GLORY."* God replied in verses 20-23:

> **EXODUS 33:20-23**
> **20** . . . Thou canst not see my face: for there shall no man see me, and live.
> **21** And the Lord said, Behold, there is a place by me, and thou shalt stand upon a rock:
> **22** And it shall come to pass, while my glory passeth by, that I will put thee in a clift of the rock, and will cover thee with my hand while I pass by:
> **23** And I will take away mine hand, and thou shalt see my back parts: but my face shall not be seen.

God told Moses, "I'll manifest My Presence to you. You cannot see My face and live, so I'll cover you up and walk past you and you can see My back parts." The glory of God is His manifested Presence. In Exodus chapter 24, God showed Moses His glory as a cloud.

> **EXODUS 24:15-18**
> **15** And Moses went up into the mount, and A CLOUD COVERED THE MOUNT.
> **16** And THE GLORY OF THE LORD abode upon mount Sinai, and THE CLOUD covered it six days: and the seventh day he called unto Moses out of the midst of THE CLOUD.
> **17** And the sight of THE GLORY OF THE LORD was like devouring fire on the top of the mount in the eyes of the children of Israel.
> **18** And Moses went into the midst of THE CLOUD, and gat him up into the mount. . . .

Moses was in the glory or in the manifested Presence of God.

We are sons and daughters of God. If God would show His Presence under the Old Covenant, shouldn't we expect Him to show it today? Sure He would, because we have a new and better covenant, established on better promises (Heb. 8:6).

We are enjoying benefits that Moses never knew about. Galatians 3:29 says, *"And if ye be Christ's, then are ye Abraham's seed, and HEIRS according to the promise."* Through the New Covenant, we are made joint-heirs with Christ (Rom. 8:17). We are redeemed from the curse (Gal. 3:13) and are now made partakers of God's blessings.

Moses was in God's Presence, and we can also be in God's Presence. If the glory could cover a mountain in the Old Testament for six days, then it is possible that the glory of God could cover our churches for six days. We can pray, and God will show us His Presence too.

It's a Fire; It's a Mist; It's the Holy Ghost!

You will find throughout the Bible many expressions of the glory of God. Sometimes it looks like a cloud or sometimes like a devouring fire, a mist, or smoke. At times the glory is even seen and experienced accompanied by an earthquake. In Exodus 24, the glory appeared like a cloud, and then it appeared to people like a devouring fire.

EXODUS 24:15-17
15 And Moses went up into the mount, and A CLOUD covered the mount.
16 And THE GLORY OF THE LORD abode upon mount Sinai, and THE CLOUD covered it six days: and the seventh day he called unto Moses out of the midst of THE CLOUD.
17 And the sight of THE GLORY OF THE LORD

was like DEVOURING FIRE on the top of the
mount in the eyes of the children of Israel.

In a later chapter, the glory was described as smoke,
fire, and even an earthquake:

EXODUS 19:18
**18 And mount Sinai was altogether on A SMOKE,
because the Lord descended upon it in FIRE: and
THE SMOKE thereof ascended as THE SMOKE of
a furnace, and the whole mount quaked greatly.**

Then Numbers 9:16,17 says that the glory was the
pillar that led the children of Israel. The glory was
manifested as a pillar of fire by night and a pillar of
cloud by day. That was the manifestation of the Presence
of God. God went with them and guided them.

Another chapter in Exodus describes the pillar of
cloud or glory:

EXODUS 40:34-38
**34 Then A CLOUD covered the tent of the
congregation, and THE GLORY OF THE LORD
filled the tabernacle.**
**35 And Moses was not able to enter into the tent
of the congregation, because THE CLOUD abode
thereon, and THE GLORY OF THE LORD filled the
tabernacle.**
**36 And when THE CLOUD was taken up from
over the tabernacle, the children of Israel went
onward in all their journeys:**
**37 But if THE CLOUD were not taken up, then they
journeyed not till the day that it was taken up.**
**38 For THE CLOUD of the Lord was upon the
tabernacle by day, and fire was on it by night, in
the sight of all the house of Israel, throughout all
their journeys.**

This glory cloud was always visible to all of the

Israelites, and they knew they were to depend on it for guidance and leading.

During the Healing Revival of the forties and fifties, people described the glory at times as a bright light which flashed. When the glory departed, every sinner was on their knees accepting Jesus. They did not know how they got there — they just found themselves kneeling before the altar, getting right with God.

I have also heard accounts about the glory manifesting like a wind that blew through an entire congregation, and every sick person was healed. If the glory of God manifested as a wind, a mist, smoke, and a bright light in the past, don't you think it will happen in this last major move of God? Sure it will!

God, Jesus, and the Holy Spirit have not changed, because they cannot change. We are on the threshold of the grandaddy of all revivals, and we can expect God to express Himself in any and all of these ways in the great revival and harvest that is coming to this earth.

Showing, Not Just Telling

In the Old Testament, God was trying to *show* His power and His existence to a world that did not believe in Him. He was eager to show Himself. We find several references where God showed Himself to entire congregations.

> **EXODUS 16:7**
> 7   And in the morning, then ye shall SEE the glory of the Lord. . . .

> **LEVITICUS 9:6**
> 6   And Moses said, This is the thing which the Lord commanded that ye should do: and the glory of the Lord shall APPEAR unto you.

LEVITICUS 9:23
23 And Moses and Aaron went into the tabernacle
of the congregation, and came out, and blessed the
people: and the glory of the Lord APPEARED unto
ALL the people.

NUMBERS 14:10
10 . . . And the glory of the Lord APPEARED in the
tabernacle of the congregation before ALL the
children of Israel.

We are heading for times when *entire* congregations
will see the glory of God.

New Testament Examples

We've seen many examples of the glory of God in the
Old Testament. What about the glory in the New
Testament? Even at the birth of Jesus, God's glory was
revealed.

LUKE 2:9,11-12
9 And, lo, the angel of the Lord came upon them,
and THE GLORY OF THE LORD shone round
about them: and they were sore afraid. . . .
11 For unto you is born this day in the city of
David a Saviour, which is Christ the Lord.
12 And this shall be a sign unto you; Ye shall find
the babe wrapped in swaddling clothes, lying in a
manger.

In Matthew 17:2 when Jesus was on the Mount of
Transfiguration, the Bible says the glory of God came
on Him. The glory of God was manifested upon Jesus as
a glistening light: ". . . *and his face did shine as the sun,
and his raiment was white as the light.*"

The account in Luke 9:29-32 says that Jesus, Moses,
and Elijah were surrounded by the glory of God, and
the disciples saw it.

LUKE 9:29-32
29 And as he [Jesus] **prayed, the fashion of his**
countenance was altered, and his raiment was
WHITE and GLISTERING.
30 And, behold, there talked with him two men,
which were Moses and Elias:
31 WHO APPEARED IN GLORY, and spake of his
decease which he should accomplish at Jerusalem.
32 But Peter and they that were with him were
heavy with sleep: and when they were awake,
THEY SAW HIS GLORY, and the two men that
stood with him.

Jesus went up to a mountain to pray, and as He did,
the visible glory that was upon Him was seen by Peter
and the disciples. Mark 9:3 says, *"And his raiment*
became shining, exceeding white as snow; so as no fuller
on earth can white them."

On the day of Pentecost, the glory was revealed as a
rushing mighty wind and fire.

ACTS 2:1-3
1 And when the day of Pentecost was fully come,
they were all with one accord in one place.
2 And suddenly there came a sound from heaven
as of A RUSHING MIGHTY WIND, and it filled all
the house where they were sitting.
3 And there appeared unto them cloven tongues
LIKE AS OF FIRE, and it sat upon each of them.

Another reference to the glory of Jesus is found in
John 1:14: *"And the Word was made flesh, and dwelt*
among us, and we beheld his glory, the glory as of the
only begotten of the Father, full of grace and truth."

When Jesus started His miracle ministry, it was
accompanied by the visible sign of the glory:

"This beginning of miracles did Jesus in Cana of
Galilee, and manifested forth his glory; and his

disciples believed on him" (John 2:11).

Acts 7:55 says, *"But he, being full of the Holy Ghost, looked up stedfastly into heaven, and saw the glory of God, and Jesus standing on the right hand of God."*

The references to the resurrection of Christ also speak of the glory:

ROMANS 6:4
4 Therefore we are buried with him by baptism into death: that like as Christ was raised up from the dead by THE GLORY OF THE FATHER, even so we also should walk in newness of life.

1 TIMOTHY 3:16
16 And without controversy great is the mystery of godliness: God was manifest in the flesh, justified in the Spirit, seen of angels, preached unto the Gentiles, believed on in the world, received up into GLORY.

HEBREWS 1:3
3   Who being the brightness of his GLORY, and the express image of his person, and upholding all things by the word of his power, when he had by himself purged our sins, sat down on the right hand of the Majesty on high.

Acts 1:9 shows that at Christ's ascension, a cloud received Him out of their sight. This was most likely the cloud of glory: *"And when he had spoken these things, while they beheld, he was taken up; and a cloud received him out of their sight."*

Then two verses later in Acts 1:11, an angel said that Christ will return in the same manner in which He left — in a glory cloud: *"Which also said, Ye men of Galilee, why stand ye gazing up into heaven? this same Jesus, which is taken up from you into heaven, shall so come in like manner as ye have seen him go into heaven."*

There are several references to the Second Coming of Christ which speak of His glory:

MATTHEW 16:27
27 For the Son of man shall come in THE GLORY OF HIS FATHER with his angels; and then he shall reward every man according to his works.

MATTHEW 24:30
30 And then shall appear the sign of the Son of man in heaven: and then shall all the tribes of the earth mourn, and they shall see the Son of man coming in the clouds of heaven with power and GREAT GLORY.

MARK 13:26
26 And then shall they see the Son of man coming in the clouds with great power and GLORY.

LUKE 21:27
27 And then shall they see the Son of man coming in a cloud with power and GREAT GLORY.

And even the reference to the catching away of the saints refers to a cloud, most likely a manifestation of the glory of God, in First Thessalonians 4:17: *"Then we which are alive and remain shall be caught up together with them in the clouds, to meet the Lord in the air: and so shall we ever be with the Lord."*

Holy Admiration

When the glory of God comes, it does something else too. It produces a reverence or fear of the Lord. Second Chronicles 7:3 says, *"And when all of the children of Israel saw how the fire came down, and the glory of the Lord upon the house, they bowed themselves with their faces to the ground upon the pavement, and worshipped and praised the Lord. . . ."*

You have worshipped and praised God in church, but when was the last time you bowed down, and put your face to the ground in reverence to God? The Old Testament saints bowed their faces on the hard pavement! At least today most churches have carpeted sanctuaries! The glory produced such a reverence for the Lord, that the Israelites yielded themselves fully to Him.

God does not want us to be afraid of Him; He's not a bully. Yet we ought to be afraid of displeasing Him. We ought to have a reverence for God, for the Presence of God, and for the things of God. We ought to have a hesitation to do anything that would ever grieve the Spirit of God, which would lift the anointing. Probably the greatest anointing we'll ever come in contact with is when we experience the glory of God.

Life-Changing Glory

One experience with the glory of God can be life changing. Look at the example of Saul of Tarsus on the road to Damascus.

> **ACTS 9:1-9**
> **1 And Saul, yet breathing out threatenings and slaughter against the disciples of the Lord, went unto the high priest,**
> **2 And desired of him letters to Damascus to the synagogues, that if he found any of this way, whether they were men or women, he might bring them bound unto Jerusalem.**
> **3 And as he journeyed, he came near Damascus: and suddenly there SHINED ROUND ABOUT HIM A LIGHT FROM HEAVEN:**
> **4 And he fell to the earth, and heard a voice saying unto him, Saul, Saul, why persecutest thou me?**

5   And he said, Who art thou, Lord? And the Lord
said, I am Jesus whom thou persecutest: it is hard
for thee to kick against the pricks.
6   And he trembling and astonished said, Lord,
what wilt thou have me to do? And the Lord said
unto him, Arise, and go into the city, and it shall be
told thee what thou must do.
7   And the men which journeyed with him stood
speechless, hearing a voice, but seeing no man.
8   And Saul arose from the earth; and when his
eyes were opened, he saw no man: but they led
him by the hand, and brought him into Damascus.
9   And he was three days without sight, and
neither did eat nor drink.

When Paul later testified of his conversion he said,
*"And when I could not see for the glory of that light,
being led by the hand of them that were with me, I came
into Damascus"* (Acts 22:11).

One of the strongest persecutors of the Church was
dramatically changed by the glory of God! And he later
went on to write almost two-thirds of the New
Testament. When we come in contact with the glory of
God, we will never be the same.

In 1992, we were in a camp meeting at a church,
and the Lord dealt with us to minister on the subject of
the glory of God at one of the evening services. My
parents had taken some vacation time to attend that
meeting.

At the end of the message, I called for people who
needed healing in their body to come forward. The glory
of God was already beginning to manifest and a number
of people at the end of the service told me that they had
seen a white mist in the building at that time.

As I got ready to pray for the people in the healing
line, the Spirit of God told me, "There is someone here

with deterioration of the spine." As I spoke that out to the congregation, my father was the first one to come up. I knew he had had some difficulty in his neck, but I didn't know that was the diagnosis.

I started to lay hands on him, but I barely touched him, and he fell under the power of God. The Presence of God kept getting stronger and stronger throughout the entire sanctuary. Two of the ushers tried to help him up off the floor, since he was too drunk in the Spirit to walk at that time.

Suddenly I heard myself say to the ushers, "Bring him over here and have him lay hands on these other people for healing."

As my father began to lay hands on these people, they began falling under the power in every direction. My father was drunk in the Spirit on and off for the next three days. He said later that the moment hands were laid on him, he heard a loud snap, and his neck was instantly healed. The deterioration in his spine was healed!

Getting over into the glory not only brought healing to his body, but it changed the direction of his life. All of my life, my father has been a businessman. But since that time, he has been witnessing to people everywhere he has gone, leading many people to the Lord who had never been to church in their lives.

His right hand has continued to burn almost constantly since then with a healing anointing. My parents now travel all over praying for the sick with amazing healings as a result. Tumors disappear. Two men who were full of cancer and were given up to die by medical science were instantly healed when my father laid hands on them. Stepping over into the glory of God can change a person's life.

Miracle-Working Glory

In the Old Testament, God proved His existence. In the New Testament, God not only proves His existence; He also shows His mercy and compassion to a lost world.

As we approach the endtimes, you will see a parallel move of miracles and healings working together. Healing shows the mercy of God to those who want it, and miracles show God's existence to those who do not believe.

We are moving into revival. We are going to see the glory of God manifested in ways we never dreamed possible. But the greatest importance of the glory is that it will move us towards God's plan for harvest.

Filling His House With Glory

How would you like to show up at your church some Sunday morning and find the whole congregation waiting outside for a couple of hours to get into the building?

You ask what is going on and someone says, "We cannot get in! The whole place is filled with the glory of God!"

Such an occurrence would certainly raise church attendance the next Sunday. Word would travel fast. People would hear that a congregation had to wait three hours to get in the building because it was so filled with a glory cloud that no one was able to enter. People would come from far and wide to see the glory of God manifested.

A similar event happened to Moses when he tried to enter the tabernacle.

EXODUS 40:34,35
34 Then A CLOUD covered the tent of the congregation, and THE GLORY OF THE LORD filled the tabernacle.
35 And MOSES WAS NOT ABLE TO ENTER INTO THE TENT of the congregation, because THE CLOUD abode thereon, and THE GLORY OF THE LORD filled the tabernacle.

Moses could not even *get into* the tabernacle. He had to wait because the tabernacle was filled with the glory of God.

Another example of the glory of God is found at the dedication of Solomon's Temple: *". . . the house was filled with a cloud, even the house of the Lord; So that the priests could not stand to minister by reason of the cloud: for the glory of the Lord had filled the house of God"* (2 Chron. 5:13,14).

Can you imagine being in a church service where the glory is so strong, that it knocks down your pastor and associate pastor and fills the room? Yet this is precisely what happened in Solomon's Temple.

If the glory fell under the Old Covenant, how much more can we expect the glory to fall under the New Covenant!

Chapter 2
Time for Harvest

If there is anything we believers ought to be able to do, it's that we should understand the times in which we are living.

We ought to know what God is about to do before He does it. We ought to know more than the world, the newspapers, or TV reporters because we know our Creator, and we have His written Word and His Spirit.

Although in the Old Testament there were men with understanding of the times, we have more ability to discern the times than they did, because we have the Spirit of the living God within us.

> **1 CHRONICLES 12:32**
> **32 And of the children of Issachar, which were men that had UNDERSTANDING OF THE TIMES, to know what Israel ought to do; the heads of them were two hundred; and all their brethren were at their commandment.**

The Tribe of Issachar was an important tribe because they had understanding of the times. They were the ones who knew what God was doing in their particular time, and they brought that knowledge to the whole nation of Israel.

First Corinthians 10:11 says that things that happened to Israel happened as examples to us, for our admonition.

Israel was a type of the Church. If they had understanding of the times, how much more should we.

Any Time — Any Place

What about God's timing? People often say, "Well, God will do things in His time." Many people are surprised to learn that this is only partially true. For example, when it comes to the blessings of redemption, there is no set time. Anything Jesus purchased in the plan of redemption through His blood legally belongs to us *now*.

We can receive these blessings now. We do not have to wait for healing because the Bible said that we were healed 2,000 years ago by Jesus' stripes. We do not have to wait to get to Heaven to have our needs supplied.

For example, Second Corinthians 8:9 says, *"For ye know the grace of our Lord Jesus Christ, that, though he was rich, yet for your sakes he became poor, that ye through his poverty might be rich."*

God did not have any set time to save us either; He was just waiting for us to hear the Word of salvation and do something about it.

Second Peter 3:9 states: *"The Lord is not slack concerning his promise, as some men count slackness; but is longsuffering to us-ward, not willing that any should perish, but that all should come to repentance."*

We also do not have to wait for God to fill us with the Holy Ghost. The Holy Ghost was poured out on all flesh on the Day of Pentecost. God is waiting for us to receive that Gift. There is no set time for us to receive salvation, healing, deliverance, or to be filled with the Holy Ghost.

As soon as the light of God's Word comes, faith rises up in our hearts, and we can reach out to take hold of the blessings that already belong to us.

A young lady once came up to us after a service and said she was from a denomination that did not believe in being filled with the Holy Ghost. She wanted to tell me what she thought about the baptism in the Holy Spirit.

She said, "I've had some friends receive this experience, and I believe it is for today. But the way I see it, it's the plan of God for some but not for all. If He wants me filled with the Holy Spirit, He will fill me."

I said, "If you believed that way for salvation, you could have died and gone to hell while you were waiting."

We are all free moral agents. We have to take salvation by faith. We have to *do* something. Why should it be any different for healing or receiving the Holy Spirit? These blessings are all received according to our faith.

Deuteronomy 30:19 says, ". . . *choose life.* . . ." God has always left the choice to us. He redeemed us and set us free from poverty, sickness, spiritual death, fear, lack, failure, and all its side effects. He gave us *"all things that pertain unto life and godliness, through the knowledge of him that has called us to glory and virtue"* (2 Peter 1:3).

There is no set time for these blessings of redemption because the Bible says, *now* is the day of salvation (2 Cor. 6:2). However, God often does have a certain time for revivals and moves of His Spirit.

For example, Galatians 4:4 says that when the *fullness of time* had come, God sent His Son. Mark 1:15 says that *the time of God* was fulfilled. There was a set time for Jesus to go to the Cross and be raised from the dead. There was a set time for Him to go to the Father's right hand. And there are set times for revival.

Discerning the times in which we are living is important. God has appointed times for revivals, but just because there are set times for those things does not mean they will automatically happen.

Within these time frames, God prompts people to pray for these moves of God. Every revival in history can be traced back to believers who sensed God was about to do something, and they began to pray in that direction until it came to pass.

James 5:16 says, ". . . *The effectual fervent prayer of a righteous man availeth much.*" The Lord looks for people to be obedient to respond to His call to prayer. James 5:17,18 says that Elijah responded to God by praying earnestly.

> **JAMES 5:17,18**
> **17 Elias was a man subject to like passions as we are, and he prayed earnestly that it might not rain: and it rained not on the earth by the space of three years and six months.**
> **18 And he prayed again, and the heaven gave rain, and the earth brought forth her fruit.**

This refers to the account in First Kings 17:1-7, when the Lord told Elijah to tell Ahab that there would be no rain for a period of time, and it did not rain for three years. In First Kings 18:1, the Lord said He would send rain on the earth.

Years later Elijah asked the servant to look for rain, but the servant saw nothing (1 Kings 18:43). Seven times Elijah told him to look. Then the servant saw "*a little cloud out of the sea, like a man's hand*" (v. 44). The cloud then grew until ". . . *the heaven was black with clouds and wind, and there was a great rain*" (v. 45).

God had spoken, but persistent prayer had to be made even with no visible results until the fulfillment came, and the rain began to fall. James referred to this when he said that Elijah prayed and it did not rain for three and a half years. But when Elijah prayed again, the heaven gave rain and the earth brought forth her fruit (James 5:17).

That actually happened in the natural realm when it rained, but God is endeavoring to show us a spiritual truth here. If we will pray for the rain, the heavens will give the rain — the latter rain of the Holy Ghost — and the earth will bring forth fruit, which is the harvest that God has told us would come.

Balanced Nutrition

In the Bible the Church is called the Body of Christ. We all have a body; therefore, we can easily understand the significance of Jesus Christ as the Head of the Body of Christ, which is the Church.

Our bodies function better with certain nutrition. If we had not eaten fruits or vegetables for a long period of time, we would be deficient in certain vitamins and minerals. When certain foods high in those vitamins and minerals became available, we might overdo it for a certain amount of time until we balanced out our system.

We saw this happen in Eastern Europe. People who lived there could not get fruit. After the Berlin Wall came down, people flooded into West Berlin, and the first thing they did was buy all the oranges and bananas they could find. They did not have access to fruit, so when they finally were able to get some, they overdid it for awhile.

About the turn of the century, the Body of Christ lacked nutrition spiritually speaking, so believers were weak and emaciated in many areas. The Head of the Church, the Lord Jesus, knew exactly what the Body needed. So God began to pour out revivals to bring balance to the Body of Christ.

Filled to Overflowing

The first thing the Body of Christ needed was power. The full-gospel message or the message of the baptism of the Holy Ghost was not a common message at that time in the early 1900s. So God gave a group of people understanding of the times and put it in their hearts to pray for a revival of the Pentecostal experience.

As a result, a man from Topeka, Kansas, named Brother Seymour moved to California and ended up with a group praying at a place on Azusa Street. There God poured out a Pentecostal Revival that went worldwide.

During this revival, people saw the power of the Holy Spirit manifested for days at a time. It was a mighty outpouring to the Body of Christ.

Some people feel that the Pentecostal Movement died, but God does not start something and then bring it to an abrupt end. He brought balance and then the revival leveled out. Four or five major denominations came out of this revival, and God was ready to take us on to the next great move of the Holy Spirit.

Partaking of the Children's Bread

People had the full-gospel message and they were filled with the Holy Ghost, but they were still physically sick. So to bring the healing message back into the Body of Christ, God again prompted believers to pray, and He poured out a Healing Revival.

God did amazing things in this revival. Everywhere people were divinely healed of all kinds of sickness and disease. Almost anyone could get healed at any time, in any place. Even ministers who did not believe in divine healing would lay hands on the sick and blind eyes would open.

The Healing Revival lasted from 1947 to 1958. The message of healing was strong in the Body of Christ during that revival. In fact, even today you can go to almost any city and find someone who believes in divine healing and will lay hands on you and pray in faith for you to be healed. The Head of the Church supernaturally brought the message of healing to His Body on the earth.

Sanctified — But Crazy

However, generally if you wanted to get filled with the Holy Ghost, you had to go to certain denominations. But what God does for one part of the Body, He wants to do for the whole Body of Christ. So He inspired people to pray, and He poured out what was known as the Charismatic Revival of the sixties.

God knocked down denominational walls and filled anyone who was spiritually hungry with the Spirit of God. Soon there were Methodists, Episcopals, Baptists, Lutherans, Presbyterians, and Catholics who were filled with the Holy Ghost, talking in tongues, and operating in the gifts of the Spirit.

This Charismatic move brought much freedom, but many people were in denominations which were not Bible-based. If something looked and sounded good, they believed it. This opened the door to every kind of extreme teaching and false doctrine imaginable.

For example, subjects like discipleship, deliverance, prayer, and submission were taken to extremes. There was a move of the Spirit, but very little foundation in the Word.

The next thing Jesus had to do was balance out these wild believers with the only thing that could bring balance to false doctrines and extremes — teaching based on a solid foundation of the Word.

Line Upon Line

Again God inspired believers to pray and God poured out a teaching revival. We've often called it the "Faith Movement," but really it was a teaching revival with the subject of faith as its strongest message.

The teaching revival put great emphasis on the Word of God and built a strong foundation of the Word in the lives of many believers. Teachers rose to the forefront, and teaching centers were raised up all over the country.

We have been in a teaching revival for almost twenty years. We have been taught faith, healing, how to be led by the Spirit, and basic Bible doctrines.

Today, however, is the day of the pastor and the local church. We frequently hear people say, "I don't have to drive halfway across the country to get fed any more. God has given us a pastor who feeds us all the time." Teaching seminars often do not draw the crowds from distances that they once did because people are being fed so well in their own local churches.

That's what God wanted. God has reestablished the

teacher in the Body of Christ to the place where he belongs. The teaching gift was needed in the Body of Christ because there was a deficiency, but now the Church is becoming balanced. God is not finished with the teaching gift. He is just not emphasizing the teaching gift to the extent that He did at the beginning of the teaching revival.

The message of faith will always be important, too, although the emphasis may not be as strong as it was in the beginning. The Bible says we live by faith, walk by faith, and that it's impossible to please God without faith. But now it's time to add to that.

Now we are getting ready for an outpouring of the Spirit of God. By the Word of God and the witness of the Spirit of God, we can know what times we are living in now. What God is preparing us for next is the mighty harvest of souls that will lead us into the Second Coming of Jesus.

Jesus Is Coming Back

For a number of years, there was a message we did not hear a lot about. We heard it now and then, but in recent times, we are beginning to hear it everywhere. It is the message that Jesus is coming back.

Every author in the New Testament talks about the Second Coming of Jesus.

ACTS 1:9-11
9 And when he had spoken these things, while they beheld, he was taken up; and a cloud received him out of their sight.
10 And while they looked stedfastly toward heaven as he went up, behold, two men stood by them in white apparel;

> 11 Which also said, Ye men of Galilee, why stand ye gazing up into heaven? THIS SAME JESUS, which is taken up from you into heaven, SHALL SO COME in like manner as ye have seen him go into heaven.

It does not matter what anyone thinks, believes, says, preaches or teaches — Jesus is coming back. The entire Bible points to this fact. The last verse in every chapter in First Thessalonians talks about the Second Coming of Jesus.

Look at what Jesus said about His return.

> JOHN 14:1-3
> 1 Let not your heart be troubled: ye believe in God, believe also in me.
> 2 In my Father's house are many mansions: if it were not so, I would have told you. I go to prepare a place for you.
> 3 And if I go and prepare a place for you, I WILL COME AGAIN, and receive you unto myself; that where I am, there ye may be also.

Jesus said, "I'm going to get a place ready for you, and then I'm coming back to get you." Almost two thousand years have passed since He said that.

James 5:8 says, *"Be ye also patient . . . for the coming of the Lord draweth nigh."* Nigh means near or close. If it was close then, it's even closer now. Jesus is going to come back and take us home.

Jesus could come back tonight. But notice He said in verse 7, *"Be patient therefore, brethren, unto the coming of the Lord. Behold, the husbandman waiteth. . . ."* We, the Church, ought to stay ready for His coming. He may not come back for quite a while, but we ought to live like He's coming back in the next fifteen seconds.

No matter how good it is down here, it's going to be better in Heaven. Paul said, *"For I am in a straight betwixt two, having a desire to depart, and be with Christ; which is far better"* (Phil. 1:23). Paul said to depart is *far better*, and he should know, because he'd been there!

Most scholars agree that Paul was talking about himself when he said: *"I knew a man in Christ above fourteen years ago, (whether in the body, I cannot tell; or whether out of the body I cannot tell: God knoweth;) such an one caught up to the third heaven"* (2 Cor. 12:2).

Paul said, "I'm having trouble staying down here in this earthly body on this earthly planet because Heaven is far better."

No matter how good it is down here, Heaven is far better. Heaven has streets of gold; we don't. If we did, someone would steal them! We have a better place to go. Our part is to stay ready.

Concerning the return of Jesus, what is God waiting for? Is He waiting for Russia to attack Israel? Is He waiting for the European community to get set up, and the antichrist to rise into power? No, those are only signs of the times; they let us know where we are in time and in God's time frame.

Is God waiting for the precious fruit of Africa? India? Europe? No, God is waiting for the precious fruit of the whole *earth*. God is waiting for a harvest of souls before Jesus returns. Once we see harvest start, we can get excited because it means Jesus is coming soon.

God Is the Best Farmer

One of the best scriptures which shows the heartbeat of God is found in James chapter 5.

JAMES 5:7,8
7 Be patient therefore, brethren, unto the coming
of the Lord. Behold, the husbandman waiteth for
the precious fruit of the earth, and hath long
patience for it, until he receive the early and latter
rain.
8 Be ye also patient; stablish your hearts: for the
coming of the Lord draweth nigh.

Throughout the Bible there are many wonderful
names used to describe God. For example, Jehovah
Rapha and Jehovah Jirah describe different aspects of
His redemption. Every name for God describes a part of
His personality or nature.

But when it comes to the Second Coming of Jesus,
did you notice what God calls Himself? In James 5, He
refers to Himself as the "husbandman." That's not clear
to us, but in modern English, it means farmer. Why
does God call Himself the farmer in relation to the
Second Coming of Jesus?

The reason any farmer plants seed is so he can reap
a harvest. *"God so loved the world that he gave his only
begotten son . . ."* (John 3:16) that He might receive
". . . many sons unto glory . . ." (Heb. 2:10). God planted
the best seed He had — His Son — Jesus, and He is not
going to quit until He reaps the greatest harvest from
His seed.

My impression of harvest used to be that God was
going to raise up a group of evangelists who would rent
large soccer stadiums and coliseums and preach Jesus
to the masses.

Those meetings are wonderful and necessary, but
there must be more to produce the harvest than that
alone. If we had fields full of wheat as far as you could
see, and we cut that wheat down and left it in the field,

would that be harvest? No, it would be waste.

Harvest is not harvest until it is brought into the barns where it can be put to use. Harvest is not a true harvest until we see the evangelistic crusades and the masses being reached.

But in the true harvest of the Lord, we also see people coming en masse into the local church, and being cared for and fed by the ministry of a local pastor. This is why God is raising up churches all over the world. Churches are like barns. God is getting the barns ready for harvest.

You Cannot Stop Harvest Once You Start

Since harvest precedes the return of Jesus, the most important thing to keep our eyes on is the harvest.

I had a friend who worked in the wheat fields in Kansas. He once told me, "At harvest time, we would unload the combines off the trucks and get all the equipment ready to go at any moment. One fellow would go out and periodically check the grain. Finally, he would come in holding some grain in his hand and say, 'That's it. It's time!'

"When he said that, we would start up the machines, turn the headlights on, and harvest the crop 24 hours a day."

He said that once harvest started, they did not stop until it was all in the barns because they didn't want to take a chance on losing any of it. They just worked around the clock until they harvested one field, and then they would head for the next one.

God is not going to start harvest in three or four nations and then take a break. Once we see harvest start, it will not stop until it circles the globe and affects nation after nation. God is not going to take a three-year break in the middle of the harvest. It will affect everyone who has the opportunity to hear.

I do not know how long it will take to bring in the harvest. Only God knows. It could be a week, a year, ten years, or twenty years. All I know is that when harvest begins, it will continue until it is finished.

The Firstfruits of Harvest

A number of years ago, God put Eastern Europe on our hearts. But every time we would try to go there, we did not have peace about the timing.

In 1988 we were in a conference in Western Europe. A pastor walked up to us who had a church in Berlin and said, "We're looking forward to your being at our First Faith Conference in East Berlin. Remember, you told my associate pastor at a conference that you would be there."

I did not remember even talking to his associate pastor! We'd had open doors for years, and every time God would deal with us that it was not time for us to go. But this time this minister told us they had already advertised our attending the meeting. This was a year before the Wall came down.

We prayed and the Spirit of God said "Go." It surprised me because we could not legally be speakers at the conference. However, we could go there on a one-day pass as tourists and legally we could "greet" the people. So we would greet people for an hour at a time telling them what Paul said to the churches at Ephesians, Colossians, Thessalonians, and so forth!

The conference was held in an old Lutheran cathedral and there were 1,000 people in attendance. The government had secret-service police scattered throughout the cathedral.

We told the people, "Keep praying for your government. Look at what they have done. They've given you permission to have a faith conference, so keep praying for your leaders."

By the middle of the conference, the government officials came to the church leaders and said, "We are pleased with what you are doing; you can do it again next year." Those government officials gave the church leaders permission to hold the conference again the next year!

That took place under a Communistic government. God was already moving. We had a wonderful time. For example, in one afternoon service, people began praising God. You could not get them to stop. There were waves of the glory of God that came into that meeting.

In one meeting, there was a lady who ran down the aisle. She wanted people to know that she had been *carried* into the meeting, and now she could *run!* A man was doing toe touches and reporting that his spine was instantly healed. It was exciting!

Something was stirring in us. The place we were drawn to was Berlin. All we knew was that we wanted to stay near the Wall. As a result, we did some video tapings in West Berlin in conjunction with a church there. Those tapes were translated into Bulgarian, Czechoslovakian, Romanian, Albanian, and German, along with several other languages, and were sent all over Eastern Europe.

One man had an unusual ministry. He put a TV, a VCR, and a stack of videotapes in his trunk, and he went from Bible study to Bible study to show them. This was almost unheard of in a Communist country!

Our videotapes included 40 hours of teaching on faith, healing, the authority of the believer, praise and worship, and biblical confession. By staying close to the Wall, we were able to preach all over Eastern Europe without even going there.

And the Wall Came Tumbling Down

We asked a man in West Berlin, "What about the Wall?"

He said, "It will never come down; it's the standing symbol of Communism. If that Wall ever comes down, you can know Communism has come to a halt."

But the Wall did come down! On November 9, 1989, the headlines of worldwide newspapers said, "Berlin Wall comes down." Then governments began to fall like dominoes throughout all of Eastern Europe. Communism fell in every one of those countries.

Why did that all happen? Was it political? Economic? No, it was God! People on the other side of the Wall prayed, and God moved on the governments and everything changed. Why? For the purpose of the harvest. I do not know how long the freedom in Eastern Europe will last, but it will be long enough for God to finish what He started 2,000 years ago!

The United States of Europe

A few years ago, we were driving down the German autobahn when we noticed a royal-blue billboard with twelve yellow stars in a circle. Everywhere we went, we saw bumper stickers, T-shirts, and umbrellas with the same symbol, which resembled a flag. We soon learned that it was the flag for the European Economic Community.

On December 31, 1992, the borders came down in Europe for twelve nations. This began the new regime of the European Economic Community, which is a continuation of the old Roman Empire. Projected plans are to have one currency, one government, one military, and one leader who will most likely rule in the city of Brussels, Belgium, by the end of the century.

Economists tell us that right now the whole world is in an economic mess. This is setting the stage for someone to come in and say, "I'll put it all together and run the world for you." Economists will tell you that once this new European Economic Community gets moving, it will be the largest economic force in the world, dwarfing the United States and Japan combined. The European Economic Community will have the largest military in the world. They will rise to a place that will amaze the rest of the world.

The formation of the European Economic Community is significant. In Daniel chapter 7, Daniel had a dream with an interpretation about a beast with 10 horns.

Many Bible scholars believe that the beast with ten horns is a 10-nation system coming out of Europe, which will be the platform for the antichrist to rise to power. John saw this on the Isle of Patmos when he received the revelation of Jesus (Rev. 1:9). Europe has an important place in end-time prophecy.

I've recently read a book on Bible prophecy written in the 1960s that gave several signs which will precede the coming of the antichrist. After reading the first chapter, I thought, *Well, that's already come to pass.*

Then I read the whole book, and chapter after chapter, I realized that one-by-one these events had come to pass. This author said that one of the final signs before the rise of the antichrist to power would be a *United States of Europe*. We are closer to the end than we ever thought.

But before the antichrist rises to power, we are going to see the glory of God sweep through Europe. Since the Berlin Wall fell, hundreds of thousands of people have been born again all over Eastern Europe and the move is now sweeping into Western Europe.

A few years ago, there were many small, home Bible studies which today have grown into thriving churches. I believe harvest has already begun! But the best and the greatest part of harvest lies just ahead of us.

We are going to see millions of people swept into the Kingdom of God in city after city and nation after nation before this last move is complete. But we have a part to play.

God has given us the privilege of praying out His will on this earth. Now is the time to pray for revival in the world. Pray for the eyes of the lost to be opened, for laborers to be sent into the harvest fields, and pray for the rain to fall. The ground is being prepared for the greatest revival ever, and we are the generation who will see it happen.

Chapter 3
Small Rain and Great Rain

Did you realize that Jesus never told us to *pray* for the harvest? We are *waiting* for harvest, but God's Word tells us to pray for the *rain* which will bring the harvest.

ZECHARIAH 10:1
1   ASK YE of the Lord RAIN in the time of the latter rain; so the Lord shall make bright clouds, and give them SHOWERS OF RAIN, to every one grass in the field.

We can pray and Heaven can give spiritual rain, and the earth will bring forth fruit. Prayer is what brings forth the rain. We ought to be praying for rain on a regular basis for our city, our state, our nation, and the world.

But what is "rain"? The rain the Bible talks about is not literal rain; it refers to an outpouring of the Spirit of God. Hosea 6:3 says, ". . . *and he shall come unto us as the rain, as the latter and former rain unto the earth.*"

The Lord said He would come to us like rain, which means He will pour out His glory, His signs and wonders, and His very Presence as rain. The rain is simply God manifesting Himself on this earth. But what will the rain look like? What should we be expecting?

The First Great Rain

The Book of Acts gives us a picture of the early rain, or the early outpouring of the Spirit of God in the Church Age.

> **ACTS 2:16-18**
> **16 But this is that which was spoken by the prophet Joel;**
> **17 And it shall come to pass in the last days, saith God, I will POUR OUT of my Spirit upon all flesh: and your sons and your daughters shall prophesy, and your young men shall see visions, and your old men shall dream dreams:**
> **18 And on my servants and on my handmaidens I will pour out in those days of my Spirit and they shall prophesy.**

These verses refer to an outpouring of the rain, which was prophesied in Joel 2:23:

> **JOEL 2:23**
> **23 ... for he hath given you THE FORMER RAIN moderately, and he will cause to come down for you the rain, THE FORMER RAIN, and THE LATTER RAIN in the first month.**

These verses all refer to two types of rain — former and latter rain. One translation says, "former and latter rain *as at the first*." What God is saying is that the characteristics of the latter rain aren't any different than the former rain except in one important aspect.

Rain is rain. For example, the rain that falls during planting season, and the rain that falls during harvest season does not fall in different colors, textures, or styles. The color of the rain does not change because the seasons change. Blue rain does not fall in the summer and red rain in the fall.

No matter what the season, rain is always the same color. Rain also does not change texture; it is always water. It does not matter whether rain is light or heavy; it is always wet. Just because you change seasons does not mean rain changes textures or styles either.

The only difference between seasonal rains is the amount. Early rain is a soft rain which prepares the ground for planting. And the latter rain is a powerful outpouring which causes that seed to spring up and grow to bring in the harvest. So the harvest or latter rain is heavier than the early or former rain.

The latter rain will be the same as at the first, only it will be bigger, stronger, and heavier because it is the outpouring that will bring in the harvest.

A Blueprint for Revival

It is hard to plan for something you have not seen or experienced. We have not seen the harvest before, but the best way to imagine what the harvest will be like is to look at the Book of Acts. Acts is more than a history book; it is a plan or pattern for the Church to follow.

We can study past revivals, but they were not the harvest. They were outpourings of the Holy Spirit to build us up and prepare us for the harvest. But the Book of Acts was not the *harvest* either; it only told about a *planting season*. In Acts, we see a pattern for how God wants to spread the gospel.

Acts chapter 2 tells us about the Day of Pentecost. When the Church began almost 2,000 years ago, 120 people were saved and filled with Holy Ghost. God sent them to the streets, and everyone heard them speaking in their own language, declaring the works of God. The people asked, "What meaneth this?" They were all filled with wonder and amazement.

When God sent out those 120 people speaking in every known language of the day, they caught everyone's attention and thousands came to the Lord. First Corinthians 14 tells us that tongues can be used for a sign. The sign gets their attention, but the preaching of the gospel gets them saved.

> **Acts 2:41**
> **41 Then they that gladly received his word were baptized: and the same day there were added unto them about THREE THOUSAND SOULS.**

This verse says that three thousand people were born again that day. Verse 47 shows that daily more and more people were saved: *"Praising God, and having favour with all the people. And the Lord added to the church daily such as should be saved."* The rain or outpouring of the Spirit of God caused an increase in salvations.

Miracles Bring the Multitudes

Another example of the outpouring of the rain of the Holy Spirit is found in Acts 3:1-10:

> **Acts 3:1-10**
> **1   Now Peter and John went up together into the temple at the hour of prayer, being the ninth hour.**
> **2   And a certain man lame from his mother's womb was carried, whom they laid daily at the gate of the temple which is called Beautiful, to ask alms of them that entered into the temple;**
> **3   Who seeing Peter and John about to go into the temple asked an alms.**
> **4   And Peter, fastening his eyes upon him with John, said, Look on us.**
> **5   And he gave heed unto them, expecting to receive something of them.**
> **6   Then Peter said, Silver and gold have I none; but such as I have give I thee: In the name of Jesus Christ of Nazareth rise up and walk.**
> **7   And he took him by the right hand, and lifted him up: and immediately his feet and ankle bones received strength.**

8 And he leaping up stood, and walked, and entered with them into the temple, walking, and leaping, and praising God.
9 And all the people saw him walking and praising God:
10 And they knew that it was he which sat for alms at the Beautiful gate of the temple: and they were filled with wonder and amazement at that which had happened unto him.

The Bible explains that when the man at the Gate called Beautiful was healed, Peter followed him into the Temple and preached about the death, burial, and resurrection of Jesus. As a result, 5,000 men were born again. That was only the first week of the beginning of the Church.

Initially, 120 people were saved on the Day of Pentecost, followed by 3,000. Then 5,000 in the Temple were saved after Peter preached. That comes to a minimum of 8,120 people in the first week of the Church in one city!

If planting season could reach 8,120 in one city in one week, can you imagine what the whole harvest will look like? For example, just in this one account in Acts chapter 5, it says that multitudes were saved.

ACTS 5:12-14
12 And by the hands of the apostles were many signs and wonders wrought among the people; and they were all with one accord in Solomon's porch.
13 And of the rest durst no man join himself to them: but the people magnified them.
14 And believers were THE MORE ADDED TO THE LORD, MULTITUDES both of men and women.

How many people were added to the Church — six or eight a week? No. *Multitudes* were saved!

Multitudes were brought into the Church by the miracles that they witnessed. What happened when the signs and wonders started flowing? When the rain of the Holy Spirit began to fall as the gospel was preached, more and more believers were added to the Church.

We see this in Acts chapter 8.

ACTS 8:5-8
5   Then Philip went down to the city of Samaria, and preached Christ unto them.
6   And THE PEOPLE WITH ONE ACCORD GAVE HEED TO THOSE THINGS WHICH PHILIP SPAKE, hearing and seeing the miracles which he did.
7   For unclean spirits, crying with loud voice, came out of many that were possessed with them: and many taken with palsies, and that were lame were healed.
8   And there was GREAT JOY in that city.

What produces great joy? People being born again! What produced these new births? People hearing the preaching about the death, burial, and resurrection of Christ. What brought them to hear the preaching of Christ? Something that caught their attention — God manifesting Himself through miracles.

ACTS 9:32-35
32 And it came to pass, as Peter passed throughout all quarters, he came down also to the saints which dwelt at Lydda.
33 And there he found a certain man named Aeneas, which had kept his bed eight years, and was sick of the palsy.
34 And Peter said unto him, Aeneas, Jesus Christ maketh thee whole: arise, and make thy bed. AND HE AROSE IMMEDIATELY.
35 And ALL THAT DWELT AT LYDDA AND SARON saw him, and TURNED TO THE LORD.

Here is a man who had been sick in bed for eight years. The power of God raised him from his sickbed, and everyone in the surrounding towns heard about it. They came to hear the good news.

Who turned to the Lord? All the people who dwelled at Lydda and Saron. One man received healing, and people in two cities came to the Lord!

People came to hear the preaching and teaching, but what caught their attention? The signs, wonders and miracles, the rain of the Holy Ghost.

The Unfinished Story

If what took place in the Book of Acts was the early rain of the Holy Spirit for planting season, imagine what the latter or harvest rain will be like!

Multiplying the signs and wonders we read about in the Book of Acts by the hundreds of thousands — spread worldwide — will give us an idea of the coming end-time harvest. By comparison, the miracles in the Book of Acts will seem small in number compared to the worldwide harvest that is coming.

Someone once said that the Book of Acts is the only Book in the New Testament that was never finished. There are 28 chapters, but we are living in the 29th chapter. The Church of the Lord Jesus Christ in our day is going to finish writing the Book of Acts!

The formal title of the Book of Acts is "The Acts of the Apostles," but do you realize that this must be a mistranslation? It cannot be the *acts* of the *apostles* because many of the miracles that were done throughout the Book of Acts were not done by apostles; they were performed by laymen or other fivefold ministry gifts.

For example, Philip who preached Christ in the City of Samaria was not an apostle; he was an evangelist (Acts 8:5). Ananias, who laid hands on Paul (Acts 9:10-17), was not an apostle; he was a disciple who lived at Damascus. Steven did great signs and wonders among the people and was the first martyr, but he was not an apostle; he was a deacon (Acts 6:5-8).

This Book should be called "The Acts of the Holy Ghost through the Church." We are the same Church, the same Body, and we are filled with the same Holy Ghost as they were. The gifts of the Spirit moved through the Church, the Body of Christ, not just through the apostles' ministry.

If we go back to the Book of Acts and see what brought people to Jesus, then we will have a good idea what God will use in these last days. God confines His actions to His Word. We do not want to be legalistic, but God has given us a blueprint to follow, and He will stay within the boundaries of that blueprint — His Word.

What Is the Difference?

What is the difference between the days of the Early Church in the Book of Acts and today? What caused people to be saved in the Book of Acts?

In one day alone three thousand were saved. A couple of days later five thousand people were saved. *". . . the Lord added to the church daily such as should be saved"* (Acts 2:47). Great miracles brought about great salvations.

Someone once said that the church at Ephesus at one time included more than 30,000 members. Multitudes were being born again, added to the Lord continually, and were filled with the Holy Ghost.

Why don't we have more results and growth like this in the Church today? Why don't we find multitudes coming to our Sunday morning services? What did they have back then that we don't have today?

Did they have a better gospel? Did they have a better Jesus? Did they have a stronger God? Did they have a better Holy Ghost than we have? No. We know from the Word that Jesus, the Holy Spirit, and God are the same today as they were then.

Could they communicate the gospel better than we can? Did they have better satellites, radios, and TVs? Did they have more books printed, more cassette and video tapes, printing presses, or Bibles? No!

Back in those days, they did not even have the written Word, much less satellites, cassette tapes, or videos. We have it all — satellites, radio, TV, books, tapes, and Bibles. We are in far better shape than they were in our ability to communicate about the gospel of Jesus Christ.

If we judged by transportation, communication, and equipment, we should have 10,000 times the results on a worldwide basis that they ever had. But we don't. What is the difference between the Book of Acts and today?

The only difference between what the Early Church experienced and what we are experiencing today is in the manifestations of the Spirit of God. They had the early rain — the outpouring of the Spirit of God with signs, wonders, and miracles. And we are heading for the same kind of glorious outpouring again — only it is the latter rain of the Holy Ghost.

Chapter 4
Holy Ghost Advertising

Have you ever been driving down the highway and all of a sudden a twenty-foot billboard with a full-size picture of a big, juicy cheeseburger caught your eye?

You probably did not even think about the fact that it was lunchtime or that you were hungry, because your mind was on other things. But instantly your stomach said, "I'm hungry; it's time to eat. Stop and find a restaurant."

You did not realize you were hungry until you saw the sign. The sign was designed to make you hungry, and the better the sign is designed, the hungrier you will become. The sign, however, does not feed you; it just tells you that you are hungry and tells you where to go to get food.

God is in the sign business. Signs and wonders are God's billboards. Signs are simply designed to get people's attention. Signs do not necessarily get people saved. After God gets their attention, then they hear the gospel and they get saved.

What are signs and wonders? Signs and wonders are not spooky. Signs and wonders are a result of the manifestation of one or more of the nine gifts of the Spirit. The Holy Ghost manifests Himself in signs and wonders as He wills as a means to get people's attention.

Divine Demonstrations

It's the demonstrations of the Holy Spirit with power that get people's attention.

1 CORINTHIANS 2:4,5
**4   And my speech and my preaching was not with
enticing words of man's wisdom, but IN
DEMONSTRATION OF THE SPIRIT AND OF
POWER:**
**5   That your faith should not stand in the wisdom
of men, but in the power of God.**

Paul always put the Word of God first (1 Tim. 2:7; 2
Tim 1:11). He put the Word first, and then the move of
the Spirit followed. In his ministry, Paul preached,
taught, and then allowed the demonstration of the
Spirit to flow to meet the needs of the people.

Everywhere Jesus went, He taught and preached
the gospel.

MATTHEW 9:35
**35 And Jesus went about all the cities and
villages, TEACHING in their synagogues, and
PREACHING THE GOSPEL of the kingdom, and
HEALING every sickness and every disease among
the people.**

If the ministry of Jesus and Paul included preaching,
teaching, and healing, then ours ought to also.

The demonstration of the Spirit and power is a
confirmation of the Word of God that has been
preached. *So the Word is the first priority*.

But there should be a balance here. If we have too
much Word without the move of the Spirit, we will dry
up. But if we have too much move of the Spirit without
the Word, we will become flaky. The Word puts faith in
people's hearts, but we still need the signs and wonders
to get people's attention.

First Corinthians 2:4 uses the phrase,
"demonstration of the Spirit and of power." Another

translation says, "but in showings off of the Holy Ghost."

The Holy Spirit has shown His power throughout history. It was quite a show when He split the Red Sea. He not only split it in two, but He also caused the water to stand up like a wall, and the Israelites walked through on dry ground. The Egyptians decided to follow them, and God closed the sea and swallowed them up.

It was flashy when fire fell from Heaven in Elijah's ministry. Elijah, the prophet, was praying, and the prophets of Baal were crying and cutting themselves in First Kings chapter 18. Elijah said, "Cry louder. Maybe your god is asleep" (v. 27).

Finally Elijah said in verse 37, "God, who answers by fire, show them *Your* power." And God manifested Himself, and fire fell from Heaven and licked up the sacrifices, the altar, and the water. Elijah demonstrated the power of God. If God showed off then, He will show off today.

Instead of the term "demonstration," another translation uses the expression, "manifestation of the Spirit and power." What does "manifestation of the Spirit" mean?

1 CORINTHIANS 12:7-10
7   But the MANIFESTATION OF THE SPIRIT is given to every man to profit withal.
8   For to one is given by the Spirit the WORD OF WISDOM; to another the WORD OF KNOWLEDGE by the same Spirit;
9   To another FAITH by the same Spirit; to another the GIFTS OF HEALING by the same Spirit;
10 To another the WORKING OF MIRACLES; to another PROPHECY; to another DISCERNING OF SPIRITS; to another DIVERS KINDS OF TONGUES; to another the INTERPRETATION OF TONGUES.

Manifestations of the Spirit are what we call the gifts of the Spirit. So what Paul was saying is "My speech and preaching was not with enticing words of man, but with the gifts of the Spirit in operation."

We need the gifts of the Spirit. There are some people, who for one reason or another, are not going to get a miracle from God any other way.

Supernatural Tongues

In 1979, Janet and I ministered in South Africa for seven weeks. One night we had a healing service with a long healing line. I laid hands on one gentlemen, and when I started to pray, I found myself speaking in other tongues.

I opened my eyes to look at the man and saw that he was staring at me. I closed my eyes in an effort to get him to close his eyes. Finally, I went on and prayed for the rest of the people.

After the service his daughter came up to me and said, "Do you remember the older gentlemen who was in the healing line? I'm his daughter. I want to ask you something. Where did you learn Latin?"

I replied, "Ma'am, I don't know how to speak Latin. I'm still working on English."

She asked, "You don't speak Latin?"

I replied, "No."

She finally said, "My Father is a Latin scholar. He reads, writes, and speaks Latin fluently. When you prayed for him, you spoke to him in perfect Latin. He understood everything you said!" God used this as a sign to reach that man!

A See-and-Hear God

The natural man cannot receive the things of the Spirit; they are foolishness to him (1 Cor. 2:14). God does not expect the world to understand spiritual things.

The world walks by sight — what they can see and hear. They are looking for a God who is alive and well and can move and change their lives today. But they cannot walk by faith, so God gives them something they *can* see and hear. For example, they can *see* divine healings.

Throughout the Book of Acts there are miracles listed that you can see and hear. For example, a blind man was healed, a man with palsy was healed, and so forth.

When God pours out His Spirit, He reaches out to the multitudes, and He will give them divine healings to see and hear because that is what will bring them into the Kingdom. But after they get saved and begin to grow spiritually, He expects them to walk by faith.

Miracles, the teaching and preaching of the gospel, and the new birth — that is God's order. We are preaching the gospel and seeing people saved, but I believe we are on the edge of seeing God manifest Himself through miracles again — signs and wonders of the Holy Spirit.

A great outpouring of the Holy Ghost is coming, and we need to be prepared for His glory. God will move in the realm of what you can see and hear, not to entertain the Church, but to reach out to the world.

There are millions of people out there hungry for God, and yet they do not even know it. We need something that will draw them in to hear the gospel. They need something they can see and hear.

They are probably not going to come and listen to a message and say, "This is great!" They may like it when they hear it, but we need something that will get them where we are or get us where they are — with power.

We only have to follow the Book of Acts to discover how many times God gave the people something to see and hear to get their attention. He will not do this for the Church as much as He will perform miracles for the world, the unsaved.

Acts 8:6 says, ". . . *hearing and seeing the miracles which he did.*" What miracles were they? Unclean spirits came out of many, and many that were sick of the palsy were healed, and the lame were healed. Did you notice when God did miracles, it was always with physical things that cannot be denied — things like palsy, paralysis, or lameness.

If someone gets healed of a stomach problem, that's good. But if someone who is lame gets healed, everyone in that place has to admit that is a notable miracle. Thank God for internal healings, but when God is doing signs, He will do things that everyone can see that cannot be denied.

We have tried everything possible with our own effort to have revival; however, it is not by might, but by the Spirit of God (Zech. 4:6). We are getting ready for another mighty outpouring of the Holy Ghost.

Healing Is the Dinner Bell

There is a lot of speculation in the Body of Christ about what signs and wonders will be like in these last days. But we have to stay scriptural. These signs will not be spooky.

Most of the time, these signs will be what God did back in the Book of Acts. The greatest and most common sign was and will be different kinds of divine healings. Healing is the dinner bell for the gospel. You ring the bell and people will come running.

Divine healing is one of the proofs of the resurrection of the Lord Jesus. No wonder the devil has fought divine healing for so many years. God will do some things in a sovereign or spectacular way.

We may as well get ready for it! For example, we will see people come in off the street who do not know anything about faith, and God will heal them in a spectacular way.

Holy Ghost Vessels

We are on the threshold of a move of God when people are going to come from far and wide to get to our churches. Not just the fivefold ministry, but the entire Body of Christ will be involved. Believers will be getting people born again, laying hands on the sick and seeing them recover, and getting people filled with the Holy Ghost. It's time for the saints to say, "Here I am, Lord. Use me!"

Some of the greatest miracles that took place in the Book of Acts did not take place in a church service — they took place out in the streets. People were going everywhere preaching the gospel, the Lord working together with them confirming His Word with signs following.

This next move will be too big to keep within the four walls of the church. The Church will have to be prepared to take what we have out to where the people are.

In the natural, when harvest season hits, everyone gets involved. Men, women, and children — they all have a part. When God starts pouring out the rain, there will be work for everyone.

Someone may say, "But I am not called to preach." God needs everyone to be involved — not just preachers. We may not all be called to a pulpit ministry, but we are all called to preach or proclaim the gospel. There is no such thing as a "nobody" in the Body of Christ. We are all equally important. As believers, we are supposed to take the good news of Jesus Christ to everyone we can.

Signs Follow Believers

God has equipped all believers with supernatural calling cards. We can go out boldly preaching and teaching about the Lord Jesus Christ and that salvation belongs to everyone.

Then these supernatural signs will follow those who believe:

> **MARK 16:17,18**
> **17 . . . In my name shall they CAST OUT DEVILS; they shall SPEAK WITH NEW TONGUES;**
> **18 They shall TAKE UP SERPENTS; and if they drink any thing, IT SHALL NOT HURT THEM; they shall LAY HANDS ON THE SICK, and they shall recover.**

God will need believers laying hands on the sick in Jesus' Name to get them healed whether it's on the job, in the shopping malls, or in the grocery stores. We need to see God moving, not only in our churches, but also out where the people are. When God starts moving, it will get their attention.

We heard about a group of believers from a church in Europe who went witnessing on the streets. They found someone who was sick and laid hands on him. It was a person who had most of his stomach removed. The man's stomach was miraculously replaced. God created a new one instantly!

You ask, "Was it an apostle or prophet who prayed for the person?" No, it was a believer operating on Mark 16, laying hands on the sick. God worked a miracle. Talk about getting someone's attention! That church is now growing by leaps and bounds. Why? Because people are taking the good news of Jesus Christ to where people are, and they are laying hands on the sick.

We all need to ask, "God, what do You want me to do? Do You want me to clean the church, be a greeter, or go to the nations?" We need to have the attitude, "I don't care what it is or where it is, God. You know what I will enjoy better than I do."

People ask, "But what if He calls me to go to the Congo?" Where God sends you, He graces you to enjoy! God has given believers authority on this earth, so He depends on us to do our part.

People Hungry for God

We ministered on healing in a meeting in Sofia, Bulgaria, a few years ago. About three hundred and fifty people were crammed in an old, dark church building. This was one of the government buildings that had been given back to the church.

I spoke on healing and that God does not want us sick; He wants us well. At the end of the service I asked the people to thank God because healing is not a promise, it's a fact — He provided it 2,000 years ago. By

Jesus' stripes we *were* healed. They all stood to their feet and praised God.

I thought I'd let them praise God for a few seconds, and then we would pray for the sick. But I discovered that if you lock people away from God for 50 years and turn them loose, when they praise God, you cannot get them to stop.

The praise kept getting stronger and stronger, and soon it was like thunder in that old church. The power of God started sweeping back and forth like waves.

People were being healed all over the building! I never laid hands on anyone that night for healing because I did not need to. People were healed all over the building, one after the other, like popcorn popping. Their countenance changed as they praised God.

Without thinking I heard myself say, "There's someone here who hasn't been able to raise his or her arms for years. Step out into the aisle and raise your arms." I could not see anyone move.

Then I heard myself say, "There's someone else here who has injured his back. Step out into the aisle and touch your toes, in the Name of Jesus."

All of a sudden a woman about 60 years old came running down the aisle. She turned around with a big grin on her face and began raising her hands. Then another woman came running down the aisle and stood next to the first woman and began doing toe touches.

The pastor told me later that those two ladies were sisters. They raised a nephew who came to the church, was born again, and filled with the Holy Ghost. He had a strong call to the ministry, and was called to preach.

This young man went back and told his aunts that he was called to the ministry, and they said, "You are not doing any such thing! We raised you, and you are going to do what we tell you, and that's all there is to it." They were not going to let him go into the ministry.

Somehow he was able to convince them to come to the service that night. Of course they sat on the back row. The power of God swept throughout that church and healed both of them.

After the service, they found their nephew, and said, "You go ahead and do whatever God tells you to do. This is real! You go ahead and preach this gospel." God healed those ladies as a sign to them, and as a result, the young man was free to obey God.

There are people who are looking for Good News. There are people who are lying in bed at night crying out to God saying, "God, there has to be a better way!" There are people committing suicide or are ready to because they do not think there is an answer.

We have the answer here in sixty-six Books of the Bible. We have the Good News, the power of God, and divine healing. We have it all. But we need something to get their attention. What is it going to take? Signs and wonders! The glory of God in demonstration.

Healings Show God's Mercy

Under the Old Testament, there were a lot of miracles. For example, the axe head that swam and fire that came down from Heaven.

But under the New Testament what do we see? Healings. Why? Because under the Old Testament, God was proving His existence and power to people. Under the New Testament God is proving His love and mercy to people.

What is God going to show us in these last days more than anything? His love and compassion. How? Through divine healings. Healing shows the mercy of God. Jesus had compassion on the multitudes and healed their sick.

Sometimes God will reach out to the worst sinners, save them and instantly heal them just to let them know He loves them. They did not get their healing on their own faith because they did not know anything about faith. God just reached out with His mercy to heal them.

Tailor-Made Signs

On our second visit to Liberec, Czech Republic, the pastor told us there was a woman in the church who wanted to talk to us.

Through the interpreter, she gave us her testimony:

> A year and a half ago, you had a meeting at the amphitheater. I was a school teacher under the Communist system.
>
> That doesn't mean a lot to you in America, but under the Communist system, school teachers were some of the most important people in the nation. A school teacher had to be a dedicated atheist and a committed Communist because the government knew it was your job to make sure the next generation was Communist too.
>
> My husband and I heard about your gospel meeting, and my husband decided he wanted to go. I didn't want to hear about any of this 'God stuff.' But he just kept bothering me until I finally agreed to go with him.
>
> We sat in the meeting and heard you preach about Jesus. I sat there thinking, I don't agree with any of this — I'm an atheist. At the end you

gave an altar call and I stood up because I didn't
want to be the only one not standing. I didn't want
to be conspicuous, but I didn't pray that prayer. I
was ready to get out of there.

Then you started praying for the sick. The
minute you laid hands on people, they would fall
down on the platform. That got my attention. I told
my husband, 'I don't know what he's doing up
there, but if I could look him in the eyes, I could
tell you.'

Somehow my husband talked me into getting
into that healing line. I got in the healing line and
braced myself. I thought you were knocking those
people down, but I decided that you were not going
to push me to the floor! All I know is that when
you walked by me, you touched my forehead, and
suddenly I was on the floor.

When I opened my eyes and realized I was on
the floor, I was mad. To make matters worse,
several young people were kneeling down over me,
praying for me. I tried to get up, but I was glued to
the floor. I didn't want to be there. My husband
had talked me into it, and I had all these people
around me. I was mad.

Finally, I was able to get up, and I grabbed my
husband and said, 'Let's get out of here.' All the
way home, I nagged at him for dragging me to that
meeting.

My head was turned because I was looking
right at him. All of a sudden I thought, Wait a
minute! My neck had been stiff for years! God
healed me while I was on the floor, and I didn't
even know it. That got my attention!

The next Sunday I went back to that church
and was born again. The following Sunday I went
back again and was filled with the Holy Ghost.
Now I'm very active in the church. I'm the director
of the First Christian School in the Czech
Republic.

**God performed one sign, and by doing that He
raised up a leader for the school. She heard the**

preaching of the Word, but what attracted her to the gospel was the sign that God performed on her behalf.

Evidence of God's Love

Several years ago, we were in a little church in the country. Again God demonstrated His power through a sign. I noticed six people sitting on the front row that I had not seen the night before. At that time, I just figured they were church people and did not think anything about it.

I ministered the Word and taught on divine healing and faith. As I reached the end of the service, I was ready to close the meeting. I had not planned to pray for the sick until Wednesday night — the last night of the meeting. This was Monday night.

As I was ready to close the service, the Spirit of God began to manifest Himself through the gifts of the Spirit. The Spirit of God said to me, "There's someone here whose last two fingers on the left hand do not work right. I want to heal him." I spoke that out.

Someone from the front row stood up and walked over and said, "That's me."

I said, "Okay," and I laid hands on him, and God healed him instantly. The man went back to his seat healed.

I was ready to close the service, and the Spirit of God started to move again. I called out another healing, and another person from this front row came up and was healed.

The word of knowledge operated six times, and all six of those signs were for those six people sitting on the front row. God healed every one of them.

I discovered later that those people had never been in a church like that in their lives. They were visitors from a church across town that preached against divine healing.

Someone had invited them to attend our services, and God did some things for them as a sign to let them know that divine healing is for today. He let them know that there was more to the gospel than what they had been hearing.

God will do some things as a sign to people. God will do some things as signs for unbelievers. He will do some things as a sign to a church body. God is in the sign business, and He delights in manifesting His power and mercy to draw people to Himself.

But there is something we can do to enhance the manifestation of God's power and mercy. If God is going to pour out His glory — the rain of His Spirit in these last days — there are things that will help produce the rain, which will draw in the harvest.

Chapter 5
God Moves Where He Is Invited

In a meeting a number of years ago, I heard a minister teach on the glory of God. He said, "Over the last 30 years, I've traveled to hundreds of churches. In all these years, I've only been in two churches where God could do exactly what He wanted to do."

"In those churches, I would plan on ministering in a certain direction, and I would no more step into the pulpit, then the Spirit of God would move. Most of the time, seven of the nine gifts of the Spirit were in operation. People were healed, ministered to, delivered, and set free."

"I would try to preach, but there was such a demand on the gifts of the Spirit, the service would last for hours. Sometimes every member of the church would be ministered to by the Holy Ghost, and people were born again and filled with the Holy Spirit."

He continued, "I'd leave there so excited about the move of the Spirit, that I could not wait to get to the next church. I'd get to the next pulpit and feel like somebody threw a bucket of cold water on me. In two week's time if we had a weak tongue and a weaker interpretation, we were doing good."

"I finally asked God, 'Dear Lord, where did I go wrong? Why was it in one church You moved through the whole meeting. In the next church, if I went by what I saw, I would think I was backslidden. Nothing would happen — no words of knowledge, or discerning of spirits. Nothing! Where did I miss it?'"

"I thought, *I'm no different in that one church than I was in that other. In fact, if anything, I'm more prepared for the second meeting than I was the first. I've done twice as much praying and twice as much studying the Bible, twice as much meditating on the Word, and far more fasting.*"

"I thought, *If it depended on what I did, I did twice as much preparation for the second meeting than the first one. If it were up to me, why was the first meeting so strong and the second meeting so much different?*"

The minister said, "I finally saw it. The difference was in the people. The move of the Spirit depended on what the people *desired* and *expected*. At that first church, the people believed in the gifts of the Spirit and desired and expected them. At the second church, they weren't desiring or expecting anything, and the gifts of the Spirit rarely manifested."

The difference is in what we desire and what we expect. We thought for years that we should sit back and wait to see what God would do, because First Corinthians 12:11 says these gifts operate as *God wills*. Yet First Corinthians 12:31 says, *"But COVET earnestly the best gifts. . . ."*

This is the same author, the same letter, written to the same church, in the same chapter. Two chapters later, First Corinthians 14:1 also says, *"Follow after charity, and DESIRE spiritual gifts. . . ."*

In First Corinthians 12:11, Paul says the gifts operate as God wills, but in these other verses he says to desire and covet them. Did Paul get confused part way through his writing?

No. These gifts operate as God wills, but Paul is telling the Church to desire and covet them. Why should we desire and covet them if we have nothing to do with it — if they only operate when God wants them to? Because God moves where He is desired and invited, and where people want Him to move.

A Wide Spectrum of Churches

As we have traveled through the years, we also have noticed that spiritually speaking there is a wide spectrum of churches.

There are churches where the minute you stand in the pulpit, the Spirit of God begins to move. There are churches where the Spirit of God moves fairly regularly. Then there are churches where the Spirit of God will move every now and then.

But then there are churches at the other end of the spectrum, where if the Spirit of God ever moved, the congregation would all run out of the church afraid!

What determines the move of the Spirit of God in these churches? Does God say, "I like this bunch over here, and I'm going to move all the time. But there's something about that bunch down there. I just don't like them"?

Is God a respecter of churches? No, churches are made up of people, and God is no respecter of persons. Does God change from church to church? No, He said, *"I am the Lord, I change not"* (Mal. 3:6).

Does Jesus change from church to church? No, He's the same yesterday, today, and forever (Heb. 13:8). Does the Holy Ghost change? No.

Who changes then?

There's only one group left. If God does not change, Jesus does not change, and the Holy Ghost does not change, then the Church is the one that has to change. The difference in these different kinds of churches is not the Father, Son, or Holy Ghost. The difference is the *people* and whether they are filled with lethargy or expectancy.

Some churches do not desire spiritual gifts. They do not even know they are for today, so the Holy Spirit never moves there.

Then there are churches that would like to have the gifts in manifestation every now and then, but there is not much desire among the people.

Then there are churches that want a move of God fairly regularly.

And finally there is the church where the people are hungry for a move of God.

In a spiritually hungry church, the gifts of the Spirit move at almost every service. Each service leaves a residue of expectancy, spiritual hunger, and anointing. The difference between these churches is in the *desire* of the people for the things of God.

There are meetings today in our country where hundreds of people are being healed and people say, "Look how God is using So-and-so."

God will always use people, but we need to learn to come together with such an expectancy that a strong corporate anointing is produced. At times like that, it's not just the anointing on a person, but the corporate anointing that fills the place. Entire congregations can be changed, and miracles can occur en masse.

God is not looking for great ability; He is looking for cooperation. He is looking for people who desire to see Him move.

The Pastor Cannot Pull the Whole Load

In writing about spiritual gifts, did you notice that Paul did not write to the pastor at Corinth? He did not say, "Dear pastor at the church of Corinth, you need to desire spiritual gifts" (1 Cor. 14:1). No, he wrote to the saints or the church at Corinth.

The move of the Spirit of God has as much to do with the congregation as it does with the pastor. It does not just depend on what the pastor desires. The pastor could desire the move of the Spirit 24 hours a day, but if the congregation did not hook up with God, it would not happen. The pastor cannot pull the whole load.

If a pastor wants the move of the Spirit, but a congregation is neutral about spiritual gifts, it's like trying to hook a rope onto the front of a freight train and pull it across town — it's impossible for one person to do alone.

Of course, the minister still needs to prepare and study. But he cannot go any further than the congregation will let him. He cannot go beyond what they are desiring and expecting.

But if a pastor did not want the manifestation of the gifts of the Spirit and the congregation did, the gifts would still not manifest because God will not override the authority of the pastor. If the pastor and church are both desiring and coveting the move of God, the gifts of the Spirit, and manifestations of the Holy Ghost, it's amazing what God can do.

Old Testament Glory

At the dedication of Solomon's temple, the musicians and singers were as one singing and praising

the Lord. What did they praise God about? His
goodness and mercy.

> **2 CHRONICLES 5:13,14**
> **13 . . . For he is GOOD; for his MERCY endureth
> for ever: that THEN THE HOUSE WAS FILLED
> WITH A CLOUD, even the house of the Lord;**
> **14 So that the priests could not stand to minister
> by reason of THE CLOUD: for THE GLORY OF
> THE LORD had filled the house of God.**

The congregation became as one, the glory of God
came in, and the priest could not stand to minister
because of the glory of the Lord.

Did you notice this verse did not mention anything
about the priests at first? It said, "the trumpeters and
singers were as one." It was not the *priest* who brought
the glory in; it was the *congregation*.

When the congregation became as one, singing and
praising God, the glory of God came in, the minister fell
under the power of God, and God took over. The
congregation had such a expectancy that it brought in
the glory of God.

Great Expectancy Produces
Great Manifestations

A few years ago, we were at a church for six nights,
and I planned to teach a series of six messages. The first
night when I arrived at the church, I felt dry, and I had
no unction to teach anything. I had studied, prayed, fed
on the Word, and prepared to minister.

But when I stepped on the platform, it felt like
something tangible hit me in the face. There was an air
of expectancy. That same expectancy was there each

night. For all of those six nights, I never taught a message I had planned to teach, yet there was a consistent move of the Holy Ghost all week long.

One night the glory of God came in so thick it was just like a white haze hanging over the heads of the whole congregation.

So I said, "Let's continue to worship God. If you need something from God, the Presence of God and the power of God is here. Just reach out and take whatever you need."

People lifted their hands and worshipped God. No one laid hands on anyone, yet we had testimonies for two nights of people who were healed. The Presence of God filled the place. Why?

The people were full of expectancy and were ministered to all over the congregation.

During the Healing Revival of the forties and fifties, there was a mass expectancy about God moving in the midst of the crowds of people. They might not have known a whole lot about faith as we know it today, but those people would go into those meetings and charge the place with a mass expectancy, and God would move.

The greater the degree of expectancy, the more the Spirit of God is free to manifest Himself. I believe that churches can be so charged with expectancy and the power of God, that people will come in even during the middle of the week and get healed.

In fact, the day is coming when we will have such powerful services that everyone in the place will get healed! At times we will not even have to pray for anyone. God will just sweep through the place and everyone will be healed.

More Than Praise and Worship

There is wonderful praise and worship in many of the churches where we minister. Sometimes it's so wonderful, once we get started, I could just stay in praise and worship the whole evening.

I've also seen churches with wonderful praise and worship, but they have no desire for spiritual gifts to operate. They have a wonderful time of praise, but the gifts do not operate.

Why? Because the people are not *desiring* the gifts. They do not let God to do what He wants to do because they are not hungry for God to minister as He wants.

God wants to do some things, and He is looking for a place to do them. The eyes of the Lord run to and fro throughout the whole earth, looking for people whose hearts are upright and perfect toward Him, so he can show Himself mighty (2 Chron. 16:9).

God wants to show Himself mighty to whole cities and whole areas, but He cannot do it until He finds a group of people who will let Him. How do we let Him? Through desire and expectancy.

In every one of those services where God moved, the atmosphere was charged with expectancy. Desiring the gifts provides the right atmosphere where God can do what He wants. If the atmosphere is charged with expectancy, it will increase and multiply the manifestation of the gifts of the Spirit. The people — not God — produce an atmosphere of expectancy.

Atmosphere makes all the difference in the world! Even in the natural, there is one particular thing that will cause rain to fall at any time and in any place. It's the right atmospheric conditions. If the atmosphere is right, the rain will always fall.

The same analogy applies to the gifts of the Spirit and the latter rain of the Holy Spirit. The right atmosphere will produce the manifestations of the Holy Ghost or at least enable God to move the way He wants to.

The fact that we function better in an atmosphere that has oxygen in it goes without saying. Likewise God can operate to a greater degree in certain atmospheres. We have always had the impression God can do anything He wants to do, but throughout history, the spiritual atmosphere often made the difference as to what God was free to do.

For instance, the spiritual atmosphere greatly affected the ministry of Jesus. So what affected His ministry back then will also affect His ministry today. He is the same yesterday, today, and forever. The spiritual atmosphere often made the difference in the ministry of Jesus, particularly concerning the manifestations of the Holy Ghost.

Changing the Atmosphere

In Mark 5:23, a ruler of the Synagogue named Jairus came to Jesus and said, ". . . *My little daughter lieth at the point of death: I pray thee, come and lay thy hands on her, that she may be healed; and she shall live.*"

So Jesus went with him to his house and when they arrived, the place was full of those who wept and mourned for the little girl. You can imagine what the atmosphere was like in that home.

Notice what Jesus did. The place was full of weeping, mourning, and unbelief. He needed to change the spiritual atmosphere of that place. Jesus got rid of the unbelief in that place by putting out all those that wept and mourned. He took Peter, James and John —

His faith team — and the parents into the room.

Three gifts of the Spirit were in operation in the healing of that little girl. It took working of miracles to call her spirit back into her body. Then it took special faith to keep the spirit there. And gifts of healing were in operation to heal whatever it was that took her life to begin with.

When all three of these manifestations of the Spirit were in operation, this little girl was raised from the dead.

But Jesus had to change the atmosphere to have the power of God flow unhindered. Jesus walked in, put out the unbelief, brought in the faith, changed the atmosphere, and raised the little girl from the dead.

No Mighty Works

In Mark 6:5, Jesus was in his own hometown, and the Bible says that He could do no mighty works there. When we say *mighty works*, we could substitute that by saying, "there were no gifts of the Spirit in operation."

In His hometown, Jesus could do no mighty works — no mighty deeds, no gifts of healing, no working of miracles, or gift of special faith. The only thing He could do was that He laid His hands on a few sick people and healed them.

It was not that Jesus *would* not do anything, but that He *could* not do anything. Why? Was it because God would not let Him? No. Was it that He decided not to? No. Did Jesus not like the people? No!

Mark 6:5-6 says, *"And he could there do no mighty work, save that he laid his hands upon a few sick folk, and healed them. And he marvelled because of their unbelief. . . ."* Why did Jesus marvel? Because of their unbelief.

Again, the people were in such unbelief that the Bible said that Jesus could there do no mighty work. Unbelief stops the power of God. That negative spiritual atmosphere stopped the flow of God.

Out of One Atmosphere Into Another

The Bible says that Jesus is our example. Look at how Jesus ministered to this man in Mark chapter 7.

> **MARK 7:32-35**
> **32 And they bring unto him [Jesus] one that was deaf, and had an impediment in his speech; and they beseech him to put his hands upon him.**
> **33 And HE TOOK HIM ASIDE FROM THE MULTITUDE, and put his fingers in his ears, and he spit, and he touched his tongue;**
> **34 And looking up to heaven, he sighed, and saith unto him, Eph-pha-tha, that is, Be opened.**
> **35 And STRAIGHTWAY HIS EARS WERE OPENED, and the string of his tongue was loosed, AND HE SPAKE PLAIN.**

Notice that Jesus took the deaf man aside from what? The multitude. Why? Because that multitude of people were so full of unbelief. How do we know that? Because anytime you have a multitude, you have massive needs.

But anytime you have Jesus present, you have the One with the power to meet the needs of the masses. And when you have Jesus present and nothing is happening, you can figure that the problem is mass unbelief. Otherwise, He would be healing the sick, cleansing the lepers, and setting people free. We know that's true because the Bible says that Jesus was sent to destroy the works of the devil (1 John 3:8).

The crowds brought this man to Jesus and said, "He's deaf and has an impediment in his speech. Here, put Your hands on him and do something!" They were taunting Jesus; they didn't really believe in Him.

Jesus took the man and led him aside and healed him. The man did not get his healing through his own faith; he had not heard the gospel yet. He was healed by the gifts of the Spirit in operation through Jesus.

But in order to get him healed, Jesus had to take him aside from the multitude. That multitude was embalmed with unbelief. When Jesus took him away from the multitude, the man was healed. Why? Because Jesus took him away from the unbelief, and brought him to where the gifts of the Spirit could operate. He took him from one atmosphere into another.

We see Jesus doing this same thing in another instance in the Book of Mark.

> **MARK 8:22-26**
> **22 And he** [Jesus] **cometh to Bethsaida; and they bring a blind man unto him, and besought him to touch him.**
> **23 And he took the blind man by the hand, and LED HIM OUT OF THE TOWN; and when he had spit on his eyes, and put his hands upon him, he asked him if he saw ought.**
> **24 And he looked up, and said, I see men as trees, walking.**
> **25 After that he put his hands again upon his eyes, and made him look up: and HE WAS RESTORED, and SAW EVERY MAN CLEARLY.**
> **26 And he sent him away to his house, saying, Neither go into the town, nor tell it to any in the town.**

Again there was a multitude of people and mass unbelief. Jesus took the man by the hand and led him out of town. Jesus spit on his eyes, laid hands on him, and asked him if he saw anything. The man looked up and said, *"I see men as trees, walking."*

In other words, he saw a little bit, but it still was not clear. Jesus again laid hands on him and made him look up. Then the man saw every man clearly.

Jesus told him, "Do not go back into the town. Do not even tell about your healing to anyone in the town." Notice this time Jesus did not just lead the man away from the multitude. He took him outside the city limits! He healed the man and then told him not to go back to the town or even tell anyone.

You would have thought that Jesus would have said, "Go tell everybody!" But the place was so full of unbelief, if the man had gone back to the town, the people would have talked him out of his healing!

This actually happens! Some people leave a dead, dry church and go to a church where God is moving, and get healed by the power of God. Then they go back and try to exist in a church where they teach that healing has been done away with.

Then they wonder why they cannot hold onto their healing! The devil comes and steals their healing, because they are not being fed anything except doubt and unbelief.

So in Mark chapters 5 through 8, Jesus had to change the spiritual atmosphere in order to get people healed. Jesus is the same yesterday, today and forever (Heb. 13:8). If the spiritual atmosphere affected Jesus' ministry *then*, the spiritual atmosphere will affect His ministry on this earth *today*.

There is nothing any better or more important than God and His Word. But we need to create an atmosphere where God can demonstrate His power like He wants and confirm His Word (Mark 16:15-20). People will come from miles away to get into a church where God is moving.

If we will get the proper spiritual atmosphere, we will experience the rain of God's glory. Usually there is more that God wants to do than what we let Him do. God can produce the manifestations of His Spirit, but God cannot produce the spiritual atmosphere. We can produce the spiritual atmosphere, but we cannot produce the manifestations.

God is not looking for great sacrifice; He is looking for cooperation. If we will produce the proper spiritual atmosphere, He will produce the manifestations of His Spirit.

Chapter 6
Prayer Is Essential

In the last chapter, we looked at the importance of providing the right atmosphere so God can move fully as He desires to. But prayer is also essential in creating an environment where God will move. Let's look at what prayer is and what it is not. Let's see how we can pray effectively for the rain of the Holy Spirit.

We can understand the importance of prayer by looking at Jesus' life. To get ready for a major meeting or missionary work, He prayed. He would pray all night and then have a healing crusade.

Then do you know what He did to get refreshed? He prayed all night the next night. He stayed rested and refreshed through prayer.

Yes, everyone needs to take a break now and then. But nothing will keep you more refreshed than times with the Father. Acts 3:19 says that times of refreshing come from the Presence of the Lord.

The effectiveness of Jesus' ministry was enhanced by His prayer life. John Wesley, a mighty man of prayer, once said that God is limited by our prayer life. He said it seems God can do nothing on this earth unless someone asks Him to.

Prayer is essential for God to continue His plans and purposes on this earth as He desires.

What Is Prayer?

If we understand more about prayer, we will pray more confidently and reap greater benefits. I always thought that prayer was bombarding Heaven to try to get God to do something. I thought that if you could get enough people praying hard enough, or praying the right formula, you might talk God into doing something.

But the Bible says, *"I am the Lord, I change not."* (Mal. 3:6). Prayer is not going to change God. James says that with Him there is no variableness or shadow of turning (James 1:17). God cannot change (Heb. 13:8).

If God wants to do certain things, then why doesn't He do them? For instance, why does He wake people up in the middle of the night to pray for some missionary around the world? If He wants to heal him, why doesn't He just do it? If He wants to save the nations, why doesn't He just save them (Ps. 2:8)?

God is not only holy, He is also just. He abides by His own legal rules, and legally, Satan is the god of this world (2 Cor. 4:4). God originally gave dominion of the earth to Adam, but Adam handed it over to Satan. When he did, it gave Satan a legal right to set up his kingdom all over the world.

So there are two groups of people who legally live on this earth. Man lives here legally. We live in a natural world, and as long as we have a natural human body, we belong here.

But since Adam transferred his long-term lease in the Garden of Eden to Satan, Satan and his cohorts legally exist here too. God owns everything, but that doesn't mean He can do anything He wants. He has chosen to limit Himself to His own spiritual laws.

For example, a landlord owns the apartment complex, but if someone has a lease to rent it, he cannot kick down the door any time he wants.

Prayer: A Legal Invitation

God has the power and strength to do anything He wants. There is no shortage of power on *God's* side; He's just abiding by His own rules.

Satan can never accuse God, "I cheated, but You did too," because God is full of integrity. He is holy and just.

God wants to do things here on earth, but He wants to do them legally, so He waits for an invitation. So anytime we pray, we are giving our Father a legal invitation to do what He already told us He wanted to do.

That's what prayer is all about.

Prayer is not talking God into *doing* something — it's finding out what He wants to do, and agreeing with Him. Prayer is saying, "Father, I thank You that You said, 'Ask of Me and I will give you the nations for your inheritance.' I ask You to send laborers to Romania."

You just agreed with God and gave God a legal right to send missionaries to that nation. You just invited God to come into this natural world.

When you pray, you are doing business with God, the Creator of the universe who wants to do things on this earth, but He's waiting to do it on a legal basis. He's trying to get us to pray.

God appeared to Abraham and said, "You serve Me, and I will bless you." When Abraham agreed to serve God, then God had an entrance into this world. Abraham started asking, and God started moving.

And through that one channel, He brought forth His Son, and then millions of believers all over the world. He found someone who would pray.

Prayer Versus Authority

Sometimes Christians get confused about what prayer is. There is a difference between praying and exercising authority. Prayer is talking with or communing with our Father in Jesus' Name. Authority is exercising dominion over Satan.

Satan's demons are here legally, but they have been defeated by Jesus. They are called "dethroned powers of the air" in one translation. Jesus spoiled principalities and powers. He paralyzed Satan on our behalf.

However, we can yield to them at any time, and if we do, we will allow them to be able to work against us.

Many Christians try to chase demons out of a nation or region or city, but Jesus never tried to run off demonic spirits. Paul did not run them off. Peter, James, and John did not run them off.

The apostles did not have to run off demonic spirits in order to pray and be effective in ministry. They took authority over them in the Name of Jesus, and went along preaching, teaching, and healing the sick.

Throughout the centuries, there have been major moves of God that occurred without anyone running off evil spirits. For example, during the Welsh Revivals, the Healing Revival, and the Pentecostal Revival, believers did not take much time to deal with the devil; they spent time with God.

We need to get our efforts going in the right direction — in prayer and by spending time with God. Dwelling on the power of the devil simply wastes time and only gives him glory.

It's foolish for us to think we are going to run off demons. All we have to do is use the authority we have in Christ. Exercising authority over them only takes a few words like "in the Name of Jesus."

Your words do not have to be loud or extremely fervent, just confident. By using our authority in Christ, we can get people born again and bring them into the family of God.

So our prayer ought to be for God to reach people who are in darkness and get them translated into light and out from under the devil's influence.

Praying for God's Best

Every major move of God in the past 2,000 years started with prayer. In the past when people stopped praying and became apathetic, the power and Presence of God waned in church services.

We need to pray for our personal lives, but we also need to pray for God's plan for the Church. We each can pray with an attitude of expectancy all week long for our church services like this, "Father, I just believe what You want done will be done this week in church. If You want preaching, it will be preaching. If You want teaching, it will be teaching. If you want to manifest Yourself through the gifts of the Spirit, that's what You will do."

"Thank You, Lord, every time the church doors are open, the power of God is there. Move however You want to move. We do not care how You choose to move. All we want is Your best. We believe that every time we come to church Your highest and Your best will be done."

We have a choice. We can say, "I wonder if God is going to do anything. I wonder what the pastor has to say today." Or we can come to church and say, "I wonder what Heaven has for us today."

I don't mean this wrongly, but it's not nearly as important what the *pastor* has to say, as it is what *God* has to say *through* the pastor. We can produce such an atmosphere of expectancy, that we will find the pastor saying things he did not even know he knew!

When we pray properly for our pastor, he then will become a pipe that God will pour Himself through. But producing an atmosphere of expectancy is not just up to the pastor — it's also up to the congregation to ask for the power and Presence of God through prayer.

Once while ministering in a certain church where the Spirit of God moved, we noticed that within the church there was a group of people who resisted the move of God.

Their attitude was, *We didn't have church like this where we came from.* I don't understand why they left their church to begin with if they liked it the way it was!

In order to have the glory of God manifest, we need to have the attitude, *God, do whatever You want. Who cares if it's the way we think church is supposed to be or not. We just want what You want.* We need to come to every service desiring God's best.

Praying for the Gifts

One of the things that will draw unbelievers to a local church is the rain of the Holy Spirit with accompanying signs and wonders. So one way for the church to pray is for signs and wonders just like the Early Church did.

ACTS 4:29-31
29 And now, Lord, behold their threatenings: and grant unto thy servants, that with all boldness they may speak thy word,
30 By stretching forth thine hand to heal; and that SIGNS AND WONDERS may be done by the name of thy holy child Jesus.
31 And when they had prayed, the place was shaken where they were assembled together; and they were all filled with the Holy Ghost, and they spake the Word with boldness.

The Early Church knew the power of prayer! When they prayed, the place was shaken. They prayed boldly, yet in submission to a holy God.

We can pray for the gifts to be in manifestation, but we do not have the right to say how they will manifest. We have to be careful not to order the gifts of the Spirit: "Lord, we want three words of knowledge, a discerning of spirits, and two gifts of healing. And let's have it quick!" We have no right to say, "I want this gift or that gift to operate."

Church services are not a fast-food service or a special-order place. We do not dictate to God. In fact, He does not even need our direction. All God wants is someone who will expect Him to do whatever He wants to do.

First Corinthians 12:7-10 lists the nine gifts of the Spirit or nine different ways that God will manifest Himself. Verse 11 says: *"But all these worketh that one and the selfsame Spirit, dividing to every man severally as He will."* The Bible says the gifts of the Spirit operate as *God* wills.

If God gave man the power to control the gifts of the Spirit, someone would figure a way to use the gifts for personal profit. So God in His sovereignty has determined that these operate as *He* wills. No person can control how the gifts operate.

I have heard about ministers who line people up and try to teach them how to prophecy to one another. But you cannot teach this. You cannot turn the gifts of the Spirit on or off like a light switch. We cannot control them.

Jesus Himself could not control them. If He could not, then we cannot. The servant is not greater than his master. Either the anointing is there or it isn't. But whether it is or not, it's up to the Holy Ghost as He wills. We cannot dictate when, how, or where the gifts operate, but we can follow the leading of the Holy Spirit.

What God wants is for us to come in saying, "Lord, I just want Your best. Move any way You want to. We long to see Your glory." We can put a demand on the gifts, but we cannot dictate what will happen. If we provide that kind of atmosphere, it will amaze us what God will do. When He finds a place that will provide that kind of atmosphere for Him, He will begin to move in spectacular ways.

Pray for Laborers

There are several ways the Church can pray to help usher in the glory of God. For example, the Church of the Lord Jesus Christ can pray for laborers to go into the harvest. That's scriptural.

MATTHEW 9:36-38
36 But when he saw the multitudes, he was moved with compassion on them, because they fainted, and were scattered abroad, as sheep having no shepherd.

37 Then saith he unto his disciples, The harvest truly is plenteous, but THE LABOURERS ARE FEW;
38 PRAY ye therefore the Lord of the harvest, that he will SEND FORTH LABOURERS into his harvest.

Jesus saw the people scattered like sheep. He told them to pray that the Lord of the harvest would send forth *laborers* into the harvest. That's one of the most powerful prayers the Church can pray, because laborers are the missionaries, ministers, and laypeople who are used by God to preach the gospel.

Pray for the Rain

It's the responsibility of believers to pray for the rain of the Holy Spirit.

JAMES 5:17,18
17 Elias was a man subject to like passions as we are, and he prayed earnestly that it might not rain: and it rained not on the earth by the space of three years and six months.
18 And HE PRAYED AGAIN, and THE HEAVEN GAVE RAIN, and THE EARTH BROUGHT FORTH HER FRUIT.

This passage of scripture is talking about natural rain. Elijah prayed and God brought rain to the earth. But there is also a spiritual principle here.

When we pray, Heaven will give spiritual rain and the earth will bring forth new-birth fruit. Zechariah 10:1 says, *"Ask ye of the Lord rain in the time of the latter rain. . . ."*

We should be asking God for signs and wonders and to pour out the gifts of the Spirit, not to entertain the

Church, but to reach the world. Prayer is what will bring the rain of the Holy Spirit forth.

When you pray, pray for the rain of the Holy Spirit in your church. Pray for the rain in your city, and for every church in your region and in your state. Pray for the rain all over North America. Pray for the rain of the Holy Spirit in Europe and across the world. Ask God to pour out His Spirit.

Praise: The Highest Form of Prayer

How else can we create an atmosphere for God to usher in His glory? Acts 13:2 says, *"As they ministered to the Lord. . . ."* What does the phrase, "minister to the Lord" mean? This phrase means to pray, praise, worship, and sing praises to God. As the Early Church was praising and worshipping — ministering to the Lord — God manifested Himself.

In Acts 16, Paul and Silas were beaten and put into stocks in the innermost part of the prison. At midnight they prayed and sang praises unto God, and the prisoners heard them. When they ministered to the Lord, there was a great earthquake and the foundations of the prison were shaken. The doors flew open and everyone's bands were loosed.

We can learn from that. Sometimes people come to church and say, "Well, I don't need anything." Maybe you don't need anything, but maybe the people on both sides of you do.

When two men began praying and singing praises to God, God sent an earthquake and *everyone's* bands fell off. Whether you need something or not, maybe someone else does.

When we minister to the Lord, He sends His power and glory and people are set free. Why? Because praise and worship provides an atmosphere where God can move.

Our Part

God cannot do what He designed *us* to do. He has given us the privilege of praising Him, providing the right atmosphere for Him to move, and praying for revival in the world. As we continue to be obedient to His call, He can continue to work through the prayers of the saints.

Chapter 7
Faith for the Glory

We've seen that there are several things we can do to enhance the manifestation of the glory of God. We can pray. We can provide the right atmosphere through desire and expectation and ministering to the Lord.

But there's something else that we can do in order to see the manifestation of the glory of God — we can believe God for it. We were in one church where the glory came in to manifestation one night, and many people were healed. After the service, I said to the pastor, "The glory was in the service tonight."

He said, "Yes, I know. We as a church constantly believe God for His glory to be in manifestation." And we know that church to this day has a frequent manifestation of the glory of God in their services.

In John 11:40, Jesus was talking to Martha at Lazarus' tomb, and He said, "Didn't I tell you if you believed, you would see the glory of God?" We as a church body can corporately believe God for His glory to come into manifestation in our services.

So in addition to prayer, praise and worship, the right atmosphere, and desire, we can use our faith to believe for the glory of God to come into manifestation.

We Need To Cooperate With God

We need to learn to cooperate with the Spirit of God, not try to control or dominate Him. Our motive of heart should be, "Father, whenever You want to bring in Your glory, we are ready for it. We trust You to manifest Your glory anytime You desire for Your purposes."

The more we cooperate with God, the more we are going to step into His glory. If we let that power and Presence come into our services, we will see people get healed who have not been healed any other way.

People often expect God to show His power without any involvement on our part. In Luke 8:43, Jesus was going through the crowd, and the woman with the issue of blood came and touched Him.

There was a whole crowd surrounding Jesus, and they were thronging or pressing in on Him. Why do you suppose they were all trying to touch Jesus? If they were healthy, and all their needs were met, they would not need to be pressing in to get to Jesus.

Probably many of those people needed healing. But did you notice that no one else but this woman was healed? The woman with the issue of blood was the only one. If there were more, the Bible would have told us there were more.

There was enough power there to heal everyone, because Jesus had the anointing without measure. John 3:34 says, *"For he whom God hath sent speaketh the words of God: for God giveth not the Spirit by measure unto him."*

So there was no limit to the anointing on Jesus. If Jesus would have turned to that woman and said, "My power made you whole," everyone could have said, "Why did Your power make her whole, but it didn't make me whole? I touched You too."

But Jesus cleared up the question before they asked Him about it. He said, "Daughter, your faith made you whole." Then they automatically knew why she was healed and they weren't. They were hoping and praying.

But this woman came believing and expecting, *saying*, "If I can just touch his clothes, I shall be made whole."

Matthew's account in *The Amplified Bible* says, *"For she kept saying to herself, If I only touch His garment, I shall be restored to health"* (Matt. 9:21). Her faith made a demand on that power. The power of God was there, but it took faith to release it.

Flip the Switch

A few years ago in a church service, my wife Janet went to the piano and started playing after the praise and worship team finished. She spoke into the microphone, but we couldn't hear her. She motioned for the man in the sound booth to turn up the sound.

The sound man was doing everything he knew to do, but we still couldn't hear anything she said. Someone in the front row whispered to her, "Flip the switch! Flip the switch!"

Janet didn't realize that this particular microphone had an on and off switch, so she was waiting for the sound man to turn on the microphone. In the meantime, he had turned the volume up. So when Janet finally flipped the switch, we had wall-to-wall sound all over that building!

We do the same thing with God. We say to God, "Do something. Crank up the power. I'm waiting for You to move." If we listen, we would hear God say, "Flip the switch. It's on your end!" God is waiting for us to move.

Playing Checkers With God

In a checker's game, everyone has his turn to play, and if someone moves out of turn, he is considered to be a cheater. Well, the same thing happens in our relationship with God. We wait for God to move in our churches. "Oh, God, move some way, some how."

We think, *Well, when He gets around to it, He'll move.* In other words, we are waiting for God to change. But if we are waiting for God, we are in trouble.

Some may even think, *If we pray long enough and hard enough, we will get God's arm twisted far enough so He will finally say, "All right, I'll move."*

The church world often thinks that way. They think, *If we can get the right people or enough people to pray — people who have power with God — then things will change in our church.*

For some reason in the back of our minds we think God has not heard our prayers, and that we need to bombard the gates of Heaven until He *does* hear us.

But the gates of Heaven are not locked — they are open. We don't have to talk loud; God's living inside of us. He knows our thoughts, and He sure hears our voice. It's not a matter of getting the right person to pray; it's a matter of knowing what to do.

What do we do? Go back to the checkers game. We already said that if someone moves out of turn, he is a cheater. Yet we say, "Oh God, move!" and He's saying, "It's *your* turn to move."

Only Believe

What can we do? We can all believe. Whoever heard of a believer who couldn't believe? We make our move. Then what? It's God's turn to move again. But God already made His move through the plan of redemption — Jesus' birth, death, burial, resurrection, and ascension.

Now it's our turn. We do what we can do, which is believe. Then it's God's turn again. I don't know about you, but I always like it when it gets back to God's turn to move again. I do what I can do, and then God does what He can do. What can He do? All things are possible with God.

I do the believing; He does the healing. I do the believing; He gives me divine protection. I do the believing; He gives me wisdom. All I need to do is believe what He said and cooperate with Him. Then it is His turn to move again.

Christians often want God to make two moves in a row without our moving in between. No, we have to take our turn and move to keep the game legal.

God will move through the gifts of the Spirit, because He loves people. He moves as a sign to let people know He is still in the saving and healing business. He is alive and well today.

But God cannot show His mercy and power everywhere because not everyone *wants* Him to move. He is a Gentleman. God is not forcing Himself anywhere. He's looking for places where people will let Him move.

You might ask, "Why doesn't God move in such-and-such a place?" The people in that place may not want Him to move. If He did show up, they would probably run out the front door!

In Mark chapter 9, a man came to Jesus. His son was having seizures. He brought his son to Jesus' disciples. They couldn't help him, so he went directly to Jesus.

He said to Jesus, "I went to your disciples, and they couldn't do anything. If you can do anything, have compassion on us and help us."

That's where the Church is: "If You can do something, help us. We need miracles, and we need the move of God. Lord, help us!" Jesus said in verse 23: *". . . If thou canst believe, all things are possible to him that believeth."*

The man with the problem put all the responsibility on Jesus' shoulders and said, "If you can do something, help us." Jesus was led by the Holy Ghost, and He located the problem. Jesus stopped and said, "If *you* can believe all things are possible." Jesus put the responsibility for believing back on him. The father was not believing anything. He was going to let someone else do the believing for him.

Faith Is Easy

In the *Johnson Translation*, Mark 9:23 says, *"Jesus said, 'It is not a question of whether I can do anything; rather, it is a question of whether you can believe. Anything can happen if you can believe.'"*

That man didn't say, "I'll be back in six months; I'll see if I can get my faith working." He didn't take long to make an adjustment. He cried out with tears and said, "I believe." He made a quick adjustment.

Then the man said, "I believe, but help my unbelief." In essence, he was saying, "I believe in my heart, but my head is sure giving me trouble."

Has your head ever given you trouble? Real faith is of the heart. When problems and doubts come to your head, run them out in Jesus' Name and keep faith working in your heart.

How many things are possible to a person who believes? All things. What do we have to do? Learn to operate in faith. But operating in faith is not hard; it's easy.

How are we saved? By grace through faith. We use our faith to receive the biggest miracle there is — salvation. We just need to take that same vehicle of faith and turn it in other directions — turn it toward souls and believing for God to manifest His glory.

When we drive to a meeting in a car, we don't have to use a different car to go home. That car will turn in different directions. We don't have to switch cars to go west instead of east. We take the same auto and go whatever direction we choose. Faith works the same no matter what direction we go.

The faith that saved us will also heal us and give us the wisdom of God. That same faith will work no matter where you point it. Just because you use your faith towards souls or miracles or the glory, it doesn't work differently.

So you just need to take the same basic principles of using your faith for salvation and use it to believe for the glory of God.

How Does Faith Work?

A smart coach will make sure his team practices the basics — the principles that helped them win.

Sometimes we have to go back and feed on these basics and water our foundation. In Tulsa, a man once asked us, "Have you watered the foundation of your house?"

I said, "No, we have enough stories on our house. We're not trying to get it to grow." I thought he was kidding.

He said, "I am serious. In this area, houses which have concrete slabs crack a lot because the ground is shifting and swelling. If you keep watering around the edges, everything will settle properly."

I thought, *We need to do that spiritually. If things are not settling right, we can water our foundation with the washing of the water of the Word of God.* The Word of God is given to us to "water our foundation" so our faith can be strong.

We have said all things are possible to him that believeth, but how do we believe? In Mark 11:22, Jesus said, *"Have faith in God."* Then he explained how faith works in verses 23 and 24.

> **MARK 11:23-24**
> **23 For verily I say unto you, That whosoever shall say unto this mountain, Be thou removed, and be thou cast into the sea; and shall not doubt in his heart, but shall believe that those things which he saith shall come to pass; he shall have whatsoever he saith.**
> **24 Therefore I say unto you, What things soever ye desire, when ye pray, believe that ye receive them, and ye shall have them.**

Faith will work for anyone. In Romans 3:27, Paul called faith a law. It's a law. But just like the law of gravity is a natural law, faith is a spiritual law.

For example, if ten people fall off a cliff, five of them won't fly away. Why? Because gravity works for everyone. No matter who you are, gravity will work for you. It's a law; it always works.

The Bible says that faith is a law. People say that faith does not work for anyone. That is like saying gravity does not work for everyone. Faith will work for anyone.

It does not matter who you are, or what your background is, faith will work for you.

So if you just find out how faith works, you can apply the principles in your life and get them working for you. Faith is the hand that reaches out and takes hold of what God offers.

In Mark 11:23, Jesus gave us the two basic foundations for how faith works. He said, *"Whosoever shall say."* How do you say it? You say it with your mouth.

"Shall not doubt. . . ." Where? In his heart. *"But shall believe. . . ."* Believe where? In his heart. What are the two foundations for faith? Believing in the heart and saying with the mouth.

We can see this principle at work in Romans chapter 10.

> **ROMANS 10:8-10**
> 8   But what saith it? The word is nigh thee, even in THY MOUTH, and IN THY HEART: that is, the word of faith, which we preach.
> 9   That if thou shalt confess with THY MOUTH the Lord Jesus, and shalt believe in THINE HEART that God hath raised him from the dead, thou shalt be saved.
> 10 For with THE HEART man believeth unto righteousness; and with THE MOUTH confession is made unto salvation.

Faith will operate by having the Word two places: in your mouth and in your heart. If the Word is not in both of these places, your faith is not going to work.

In fact, eight times out of ten, when our faith is not working, the problem is between our nose and chin. Putting the Word in our hearts is easy. But many people have trouble putting the Word in their mouths.

Then to keep faith working, we've got to *keep* the Word in our mouths and in our hearts.

Faith operates by putting God's Word in our hearts and our mouths. Faith works by believing and saying. Our faith will work negatively or positively. Eventually, we will receive whatever we are consistently believing and saying.

Your life is a result of what you have been believing and saying about yourself up to this point. Over time, what you believe and say about your life and yourself will come to pass because that's how faith works.

Faith works by believing and saying. If we want to see the glory of God, as a congregation we have to believe and say the right words. We have to believe for the glory of God and watch the words of our mouths.

Believing Is Easy

People sometimes say that it's hard to believe God. Did you ever hear of a believer who couldn't believe? That would be like a human being say, "I wish I could breathe. It's so hard." No, that's what you do naturally. You are a human, so you breathe. Likewise you are a believer, so you believe.

Our problem is not the believing part. We believe all the time. Anything someone tells us — we either believe it or we don't. We just make a choice. Believing is the easiest thing in the world. Our problem is not knowing *how* to believe, it's knowing *what* to believe.

In Isaiah 5:13 God said, *"Therefore my people are gone into captivity, because they have no knowledge. . . ."* God didn't say they went into captivity because they didn't have *faith*. He said they went into captivity because they did not have *knowledge*.

Hosea 4:6 says, *"My people are destroyed for lack of knowledge. . . ."* Our problem hasn't been the *lack of ability* to believe, but rather knowing *what* to believe.

We thought believing was a feeling. No, it isn't. During some of my greatest faith victories, I had no feeling whatsoever. Faith has nothing to do with feelings.

Only one thing can produce faith, and that is hearing the Word of God.

If someone asks you, "Do you believe John Smith?" I don't think you would say, "I'm trying to believe him." No, you would say, "I don't know. What did he say?" Then once you knew what John Smith said, you would make a decision whether or not you would believe him based on whether or not what he said was in the Word.

Once you know what John Smith said, then it becomes a decision and not a physical exercise or mental strain to believe what he said. The same analogy applies to believing God.

People say, "I'm trying to believe God," when they ought to be asking, "What did God say?" Believing God is the easiest thing in the world once you know what He said.

How do you know what He said? You hear it. You feed on His Word. Then you make the decision, "Am I going to believe this or not?"

Believing God means nothing more than taking time to feed on the Word of God until that Word gets inside you. Then once you hear what God says, make a decision that no matter what comes along, you are going to believe God's Word in any area of His promises — including for the glory of God to be manifested.

God's Priority Is Souls

Hebrews 10:38 says, *"Now the just shall live by faith: but if any man draw back, my soul shall have no pleasure in him."* We live by faith — that's what pleases God. We have been given the privilege of believing God for everything in life — jobs, money, clothing, food, and so on.

But we need to apply our faith beyond our own needs to God's needs. He wants us to believe for the salvation of souls, and the move of His Spirit, and for the glory of God to be demonstrated in our midst. Our faith works the same way, no matter what we are believing for.

John 11:40 says that Jesus said to Martha, *". . . Said I not unto thee, that, if thou wouldest believe, thou shouldest see the glory of God?"* When a congregation believes, God shows up to minister to the needs of the people. He said that if we believe, we will see His glory — His manifested Presence.

Let's operate in faith fully and please God with our faith. Let's believe for the glory; let's believe for souls; and let's believe for the harvest. God is depending on us to believe for His glory to be in demonstration, so He can usher in the greatest revival that the world has ever seen. And it all begins with the basic principles of faith.

Chapter 8
Flowing With the Spirit

A few years ago, I noticed that many of our services were not flowing like they should. Something didn't feel right. Often it seemed like I was running into a brick wall and ministering seemed dry. I prayed, "Lord, we are having a lot of services that are not flowing as they should. Something's wrong. What is it?"

Finally God showed me the problem. I was going in one direction, and the anointing was going in another direction.

I would study a subject, and I knew exactly what I was going to teach each night for four or five nights. Then I would get into a service and the Holy Ghost would nudge me to go in another direction. However, I would ignore that nudging and go with my own plan.

God said to me, "The problem you're running into is that you're going one direction and the anointing is going another. If you'll follow the Holy Ghost, you'll always have the Holy Ghost's plan. If you will follow My anointing, you'll always have My anointing. If you'll follow the glory, you'll always have the glory."

I realized that I needed to be more flexible in my services. I needed to have a plan, but I also had to be willing to put it aside and move with the Holy Spirit. I asked Him to show me what to do and spell it out for me in black and white. I knew He would.

God dealt with us to do some meetings with another minister who had been in the ministry longer than we had been. He was used mightily of God. We were in a large church, and I was sitting on the platform behind him. He stood up, opened up his Bible, and took out his notes. He looked at them for awhile, paused, then looked again, and soon he started walking across the platform.

A congregation of about 800 people sat there, looking at him while he continued to walk across the platform. Then he picked up his notes and looked at his Bible again without saying anything.

I thought, *What is he doing? If he doesn't have anything to teach, he should sit down. I can teach! I'm a teacher. I can always teach.*

Soon he walked back to the pulpit, stopped, looked at his Bible, and glanced around the congregation. The people were sitting there looking at him wondering, *What is this guy doing?* It seemed like thirty minutes, but it was probably only a minute or two.

Finally, he said, "Who is it? Someone in here has. . . ," and he named a particular physical problem. Someone raised his hand and the minister said, "Come up here." The person went forward and he ministered to him, and the man was healed by the power of God.

Faith in the Power of God

Just like pulling the cap out of a bottle causes everything to instantly flow out, when that minister flowed with the anointing, a cap was pulled out in the Spirit realm. And immediately the Holy Ghost began to move and the glory poured out all over the congregation.

There were instant manifestations of the gifts of the Spirit in operation, and people were healed and set free of all kinds of ailments. This lasted for about two hours. You didn't *wonder* if God was present — you *knew* He was.

In First Corinthians 2:4-5, Paul said, "*And my speech and my preaching was not with enticing words of man's wisdom, but in demonstration of the Spirit and of power: That your faith should not stand in the wisdom of men, but in the power of God.*"

Sometimes God wants to demonstrate with His power what has been preached. These demonstrations of the Spirit of God do not take *priority* over the Word of God, but they *confirm* the Word and help people understand the Word.

About that time the minister said, "Well, I'm done." And he gave the microphone back to the pastor, and headed out a side door by the platform. He motioned for me, so I followed along behind the platform. All of a sudden he stopped and turned back around. He didn't know that I had had questions about this.

Remember, I had been asking God about the move of the Spirit of God. I understood some things as far as moving with the Spirit of God, but I didn't understand *how* to do it.

I was a teacher — cut and dried, start and stop, give an altar call, lay hands on the sick — and go home. I always knew what I was going to teach five nights ahead of time.

All of a sudden the other minister stopped, turned around, looked at me and said, "Did you see that?"

I thought, *Yes, I was there, but I don't know what I saw.*

He said, "I checked, and the anointing to preach just wasn't there. So I thought I would teach. But I checked, and the anointing to teach wasn't present either."

As he said that I thought, *Boy, I've been there before and I knew what to do! When the anointing to teach isn't there and the anointing to preach isn't there, you just put your head down and push through and try to teach anyway!*

He then said, "The anointing to teach wasn't there and the anointing to preach wasn't there, so I thought, *If the anointing to teach isn't here and the anointing to preach isn't here, then the anointing must be here to do something else. We're just going to wait on God and find out what it's here for.*"

Then I began to understand the need to stop and wait for the direction of the Holy Spirit, even with 800 people watching. Before I understood this, I would have plowed full-speed ahead in my services and often it was hard to teach, but I would try anyway. There was not a smooth flow, and the people did not seem to be involved with my teaching.

Sometimes that happens because people are not hooking up with you. Either they are tired, or they don't like what you're saying. But in either case if the people don't hook up, you can't accomplish much.

But I knew it wasn't always the congregation's fault. I knew something was wrong on my part; I just didn't know what it was. When the anointing wasn't there to teach I thought, *Well, I'm a teacher; I'm going to teach anyway.* And I would just bulldoze through, never paying attention to the leading of the Holy Ghost.

But now I was beginning to understand what it meant to move with the Spirit of God. I was learning to take the time and to wait on God for direction.

I would ask the Lord questions like, "Do you want me to teach?" And if there was a check in my spirit to teach, then I would ask another question and wait on God. Finally, I was learning what it meant to be flexible to move with the Spirit of God.

Obeying the Lord

Something else I have learned is that following the leading of the Holy Spirit means you cannot gear the service toward one person unless God directs you that way.

For example, if He does not speak to you specifically to minister to a certain individual, no matter how sincere you are in wanting to meet someone's needs, you have to wait and let God move through you. Otherwise, you may be following the influence of your head and emotions rather than your spirit.

Several years ago, there was a man in the congregation who I knew needed healing. I knew exactly what I wanted to teach to help him.

I was ready to teach, and the Spirit of God began to move, so I followed Him in a different direction. When I followed His direction, the Presence of God came in and filled the room.

The Presence of God comes in different forms. Sometimes it is a hilarious presence; sometimes it is a quiet presence, but this time was different. His compassion filled the whole room. All over the congregation I saw grown men with tears running down their faces. It was not anything that was worked up, because no one had said anything.

We followed the Holy Ghost and people were healed. But at the end of the service, condemnation hit me. I began thinking thoughts like: *Boy, you blew it! You think you are following the Holy Ghost and here is a man dying with sickness in his body and you didn't teach what he needed! He's going to die, and it's going to be to your fault.*

I knew better than to listen to the lies of the devil, but sometimes you listen without thinking.

I felt like a heel, and I wanted to get out of there. I thought, *Bless his heart, that man drove a long distance to get healed!* I didn't even want to see him, I felt so bad!

Then I thought, *There's no other door. I have to pass him to get out of the building.* To make matters worse, I saw him coming up the aisle toward me. I thought, *Oh! He's going to come up and tell me how bad his physical condition is and what the doctors have said.*

About that time, I looked up and he was walking toward me with a big grin on his face. He said, "I want you to know, I got it tonight! I've never known God's love like this before. Somehow in this service, I understood God's love toward me and it changed me!"

We received word from him a couple of months later that he had gone back to the doctors and they said he didn't have a symptom left in his body!

If we will let God have His way, He will get more done in ten minutes than we could in ten years. It's not that teaching and preaching do not help people, but sometimes God wants to confirm His Word with signs and change someone's life.

Let's flow with the anointing! If the anointing isn't present to do something, it must be present to do something else. Let's find out what the anointing is present for.

People say, "Well, that doesn't apply to me. I'm not up there preaching or teaching."

If you're in the congregation, this applies to you because the congregation is just as important as the minister. The minister can pray, fast, study, read, and meditate, but if the congregation isn't willing to flow when God begins to flow, this hinders the anointing.

It's a joint effort. Everyone needs to work together; one man cannot carry the whole load. Even Jesus could do no mighty work when the congregation wouldn't cooperate with Him in His own hometown.

Types and Shadows of the Holy Spirit

Paul wrote in First Corinthians 10:11 that the things that happened to Israel happened as examples for our admonition. Israel was a type of the Church, so we can look at Israel and see how the things that happened to them apply to us.

We can learn how to flow with the Spirit of God through studying these types and shadows. One good example is found in this passage in Ezekiel.

EZEKIEL 47:1-5
1 Afterward he brought me again to the door of the house; and, behold, waters issued out from under the threshold of the house eastward: for the forefront of the house stood toward the east, and the waters came down from under the right side of the house, at the southside of the altar.
2 Then brought he me out of the way of the gate northward, and led me about the way without unto the utter gate by the way that looketh eastward; and, behold, there ran out waters on the right side.
3 And when the man that had the line in his hand went forth eastward, he measured a thousand cubits, and he brought me through the waters; the waters were to the ankles.

> 4 Again he measured a thousand, and brought
> me through the waters; the waters were to the
> knees. Again he measured a thousand, and
> brought me through; the waters were to the loins.
> 5 Afterward he measured a thousand; and it was
> a river that I could not pass over: for the waters
> were risen, waters to swim in, a river that could
> not be passed over.

The prophet Ezekiel had a vision. An angel appeared to him with a measuring rod in his hand. He took Ezekiel to a mighty river and left him by the shore, and he measured out a certain distance which would be about one-third of a mile.

Then the angel came back and took Ezekiel by the hand and walked him out where the waters were ankle deep (v. 3). He left him again and measured another one-third mile and again took him out to knee-deep waters (v. 4).

Then the angel measured out another one-third mile and the water was waist deep (v. 4). Then he measured out another one-third mile, and the water was so deep all Ezekiel could do was swim (v. 5).

The Anointing Is Like a River

There are many practical truths in these passages of Scripture that relate to the move of the Holy Spirit in these last days.

Let's say the river is the anointing. Often in the Scriptures, moving waters are a type of the move of the Spirit of God. The man with the line in his hand is an angel, but let's compare him to the Holy Ghost. The river flowing out from the altar — from the Presence of God — is the anointing or move of the Spirit.

Let's say we are at the shallow part of the river with our toes dangling in the water, and we're saying, "This is good! We are in an ankle-deep anointing!" We feel satisfied. Then the Holy Ghost comes with His measuring line in His hand to gently move us on to knee-deep waters.

Notice the angel didn't pick Ezekiel up by a lock of his hair and drop him in deep water. Ezekiel would not have known what to do.

Well, God is doing the same thing with us by the Holy Spirit. God knows that if He dropped us headfirst in the deep anointing, some of us would drown. We would not know what to do with it.

So God is going to measure out a little bit of anointing and come back, take us by the hand, take us a little farther, and let us get used to the ankle-deep anointing. As we become familiar with the ankle-deep anointing, He will measures out the next degree of knee-deep anointing.

The Holy Spirit will measure out another thousand cubits and lead us and soon we will be enjoying knee-deep anointing. Then He will take us to where we are in waist-deep anointing.

We may become satisfied and think, *Oh, this is good! Let's have a good time here*! But we can't stay there; we have to keep moving on.

The next step is the last third of a mile; He's going to lead us out to where the water is over our head and all we can do is swim in it.

I like the ankle-deep water, but I'm looking forward to swimming in that deep anointing! God is endeavoring to take us into swimming waters of the anointing of God.

He is trying to take us by the hand and lead us if we will just move with Him, flow with Him and follow Him. His leadings are not hard. His leadings will witness on the inside, and line up with the Word of God.

Ezekiel was totally dependent on the man with the measuring rod in his hand. Likewise, we are totally dependent on the Spirit of God. Learning to follow God is progressive, so we should never be discouraged if we do not learn everything overnight. The Holy Spirit will teach us a little bit at a time.

Swimming in Deep Waters

We can see what will happen when we begin to swim in those waters.

EZEKIEL 47:6-9
6 And he said unto me, Son of man, hast thou seen this? Then he brought me, and caused me to return to the brink of the river.
7 Now when I had returned, behold, at the bank of the river were very many trees on the one side and on the other.
8 Then said he unto me, These waters issue out toward the east country, and go down into the desert, and go into the SEA which being brought forth into the SEA, the waters shall be healed.
9 And it shall come to pass, that every thing that liveth, which moveth, WHITHERSOEVER THE RIVERS SHALL COME, SHALL LIVE: and there shall be a very great MULTITUDE OF FISH, because these waters shall come thither: for they SHALL BE HEALED; and EVERY THING SHALL LIVE whither the river cometh.

The first thing this scripture talks about is salvation. Oftentimes "sea" means a large group of people. He is saying that if we will move with these rivers, they will take us to the seas of the people, meaning multitudes of people who need to be born again.

The flow of the river also refers to the flow of the anointing, the deep waters where God wants us to swim. He is saying throughout these passages that if we will flow with these rivers, they are going to bring life to the multitudes — eternal life — the new birth!

It goes on to say that there shall be a great multitude of fish. This refers to the harvest! God will make us fishers of men.

The second part of verse 9 refers to healing: "*. . . because these waters shall come thither: for they shall be healed; and every thing shall live whither the river cometh.*"

Whoever comes into contact with the glory of God can be healed. God will use signs, wonders, and miracles to heal the multitudes and bring them to salvation.

God's Original Purpose

There are some things God is endeavoring to draw the Church over into, and it's not going to happen unless we follow the leading of the Holy Ghost into fresh anointings. If we follow man's plans we are in trouble. We must follow God's plans.

Throughout the Bible, God has been trying to teach us to follow His plan. What God was trying to show the people at the Tower of Babel was there is only one plan into Heaven and that's His plan — no other plan is ever going to work.

For example, Abraham decided to try his own plan and ended up with an Ishmael. Saul tried to equip David with his own armor, but David couldn't use

Saul's armor because he knew God had a different plan for him. That's why he picked up his sling, and killed the giant.

The move of the Spirit has to do with the harvest coming in these last days. We are not going to see the harvest come in like it's suppose to until we learn to flow with the plan of the Spirit of God.

Instead of following our own plan, our own stream and what we want to do, let's get in and learn to follow His stream. Then we will be swimming in the water that takes life to the multitudes and there will be great healings and salvations.

We have a choice. The river is moving, and the Holy Ghost is measuring that anointing for us. We are going to have to move with Him. Let's let Him teach us. Let's let Him take us by the hand and go. When we get used to ankle-deep water, He will take us to knee-deep water.

When we get used to knee-deep water, He will take us to waist-deep water. When we get used to waist-deep water, He will take us swimming in those rivers of water.

There is a move of God coming, and God is preparing the Church just like He was preparing Ezekiel — one step at a time. But we need to learn to be sensitive to the Spirit of God. The Holy Spirit will lead us to the glory. If we will follow the Spirit of God, He will take us on out to the rivers of His glory.

Blood, Fire, and Vapor

The Word gives us three signs that we can expect to see increasingly as the glory begins to manifest and we continue to follow the Holy Spirit in the deep waters of anointing.

In Acts 2:14, Peter quoted from the Book of Joel chapter 2 where God said He would pour out His Spirit:

ACTS 2:14
14 Ye men of Judaea, and all ye that dwell at Jerusalem, be this known unto you, and hearken to my words: For these are not drunken, as ye suppose, seeing it is but the third hour of the day. But this is that which was spoken by the prophet Joel.

JOEL 2:28,29
28 And it shall come to pass afterward, that I will pour out my spirit upon all flesh; and your sons and your daughters shall prophesy, your old men shall dream dreams, your young men shall see visions:
29 And also upon the servants and upon the handmaids in those days will I pour out my spirit.

In Acts 2:19, God lists three different signs: *"And I will shew wonders in heaven above, and signs in the earth beneath; blood, and fire, and vapour of smoke."*

Most theologians believe these verses stand for destruction, war, and bloodshed. But let's look at another possible interpretation.

The blood could stand for the blood of Jesus which refers to salvation or the new birth. The fire could stand for the outpouring of the Holy Ghost. Acts 2 says that there appeared unto them cloven tongues like as fire. This referred to the infilling of the Holy Ghost or the baptism of the Holy Ghost.

As the great revival begins and the glory is poured out, millions of people will be born again and filled with the Spirit.

The vapor of smoke could refer to the glory of God throughout the Scriptures. And the glory of the latter house shall be greater than of the former (Haggai 2:9). The glory of the early days was wonderful, but the glory that is to come will be far more glorious than we can even imagine.

God is getting us ready for something we have not yet seen. It will be exceedingly abundantly above all we can ask or think. This is not the day or the hour to be slothful. Now is the time to get fired up and be ready for what God is doing. God is raising up churches filled with believers who will preach the Word and move with the Spirit of God.

The harvest and the glory of God is coming, Church. Let's get ready! Let's prepare for God's glory!

For a complete catalog of books and tape series, or to receive Mark Brazee Ministries free bimonthly newsletter, please write to:

Mark Brazee Ministries
P. O. Box 1870
Broken Arrow, OK 74013